GORDONRAMSAY'S
SECRETS

GORDONRAMSAY'S
SECRETS

WITH **ROZ DENNY AND MARK SARGEANT**

PHOTOGRAPHS BY **GEORGIA GLYNN SMITH**

Dedication
For my youngest daughter, Matilda, born on my birthday.

First published in 2003 by
Quadrille Publishing Limited
Alhambra House
27-31 Charing Cross Road
London WC2H 0LS

This edition produced for
The Book People Ltd
Hall Wood Avenue
Haydock
St Helens WA11 9UL

Text © 2003 Gordon Ramsay
Photography © 2003 Georgia Glynn Smith
Design and layout © 2003 Quadrille Publishing Limited

Publishing director Anne Furniss
Art director Helen Lewis
Project editor Janet Illsley
Photographer Georgia Glynn Smith
Food stylist Mark Sargeant
Props stylist Jane Campsie
Production Beverley Richardson

Cataloguing in Publication Data: a catalogue record for this book is available from the British Library.

ISBN 1 84400 137 7
Printed in China

notes
• *All spoon measures are level unless otherwise stated:*
1 teaspoon = 5ml spoon; 1 tablespoon = 15ml spoon.
• *Egg sizes are specified where they are critical, otherwise you can use either large or medium eggs. I recommend free-range eggs. If you are pregnant or in a vulnerable health group, avoid those recipes that contain raw egg whites or lightly cooked eggs.*
• *Ovens should always be preheated to the specified temperature. Individual ovens can deviate by as much as 10°C from the setting, either way. Get to know your oven and use an oven thermometer to check its accuracy. My timings are provided as guidelines, with a description of colour or texture where appropriate.*

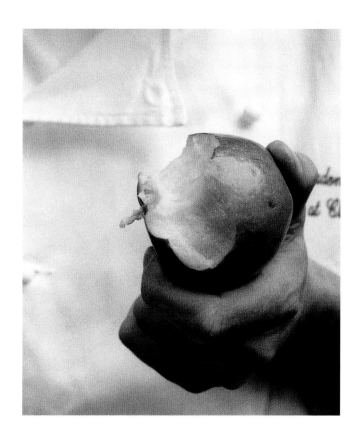

Introduction

It is 10 years since I opened my first restaurant with a kitchen brigade of four at the Aubergine restaurant, and over 15 years since I quit football and took up cooking. In that time I have learnt an incredible amount about food, and life. I have learnt from my own experiences, but most of all from others who have willingly passed on their knowledge and secrets to me. Aubergine put me on the culinary map and since becoming independent 5 years ago I now have a company that runs a number of restaurants from Dubai to Glasgow and employs hundreds of staff. It would be tempting to think this was achieved through some formula that could be broadened into a chain or franchise but there is no one magic trick, just a number of elements.

First and foremost, I am a cook, not a businessman. I won't discard my chef's jacket for a suit. And all those who work in the kitchens are cooks. They don't get bogged down with paperwork, accountants etc. I don't blur any boundaries and neither should they. Each time I open a new restaurant it has an exclusive identity and I share the responsibility for cooking with a head chef. I like to hand over to a chef who has worked alongside me for years and knows the level of skill and standards I expect. A number of my chefs have become figures in their own right: Mark Askew at the three Michelin starred Gordon Ramsay Restaurant in Chelsea; Marcus Wareing of Petrus and the Savoy Grill; Mark Sargeant at Claridges; and more recently Angela Harnett at The Connaught. I try to ensure that I spend at least one service a day – lunch or dinner – in one of the kitchens. Consistent quality is vital and the reason why I will never relax. Food is still a passion after all these years.

Not surprisingly I am sometimes asked what are the secrets of my success. Why does the cooking in my restaurants consistently receive awards? The reasons are simple – high quality ingredients, the skill and dedication of my chefs, and the techniques we use. So, in this book I want to share with you some of the secrets that have helped me along the way. I have divided the chapters according to the type of food because many of the techniques that apply – to eggs, for example – relate to each other. The idea is that each recipe illustrates a particular skill, highlights the supply of an ingredient or a special technique. Work your way through the recipes and you should greatly improve your culinary knowledge and skill. Do take the time to carefully read a recipe through, before you even make out a shopping list, to familiarise yourself with the method and equipment you might need.

You do not need a batterie of expensive tools to reproduce my recipes, but a good selection of sharpened knives is essential. There is no such thing as an all-purpose knife. At the very least you will need a large cook's knife, a small vegetable knife, a filleting knife and a boning knife. Japanese knives impress me now, their stylish designs delivering accurate precision. Similarly, good, heavy non-stick pans are vital. You cannot successfully pan-roast sweet fresh scallops at a high heat in a flimsy, thin-based pan. I reckon I must spend more than any other chef in Europe on non-stick pans. We also use top quality electric mixers and stick blenders for our light mousses, sauces and purées.

Another overall secret is my continual search for inspiration. Whenever I can, I take off for a couple of days to visit a new region of France, Italy or Spain, sample local specialities and visit one or two restaurants a day. If a dish impresses me, I don't copy it, I break it down into its basic elements and re-invent. There are no gimmicks in my recipes. Paris always inspires and brings back memories of formative years, but I am increasingly impressed with the food of Montpellier in Languedoc and Barcelona, both areas where Catalan inspired dishes are achieving new heights.

Finally, a few practical notes. Much of the fish and meat in this book is quickly cooked so it remains juicy and tender. This requires good quality produce that is correctly and hygienically stored, so buy wisely from good suppliers. Likewise, some of the dishes use lightly cooked eggs and I suggest you buy free-range, preferably organic. Measure carefully, ideally with digital scales for accurate readings. And remember that oven temperatures can only be guidelines, given that there is quite a variation between models. Check a dish a few minutes before it is supposed to come out of the oven and be prepared to allow longer if necessary. There is much more to good cooking than slavishly following instructions, even mine!

Shellfish

Most chefs will tell you that the shellfish section in a restaurant kitchen is probably their favourite. I never cease to marvel at the wonderful creatures that land on our kitchen boards each day. In fact we British chefs are quite spoilt. The cold waters around our coastline nurture fabulous plump sweet-fleshed lobsters, langoustines and scallops. A popular dish on our Aubergine menu in the mid-1990's was sautéed scallops with crispy pan-fried potatoes and a fresh cream vinaigrette. One regular high-profile customer would make a special request for 'no potatoes' in the hope we would fill the gaps on his plate with more sweet scallops. But I soon twigged and piled the salad leaves high instead.

My earliest handling of shellfish was quite different. On the shores of Loch Lomond, my Dad, brother, Ronnie, and I were in search of sea trout and salmon. But first we needed bait. This came in the form of giant wild mussels and oysters exposed as the tide went out. As an 11 year old, I struggled to prise open large obstinate oysters. I had no idea that a decade on I'd be relishing sipping the juice of oysters spiked with Tabasco and lemon.

Naturally, we buy shellfish in substantial quantities and only the best quality. I look to enhance the delicate flavours and textures of these creatures with simple poaching, steaming or quick pan-frying. Of course, freshness is paramount. The best guarantee of absolute freshness is to buy your shellfish from a reputable fishmonger with a high turnover and, whenever possible, buy live.

poached lobster with potato and rocket salad

This simple, elegant salad looks stunning. You will need two live lobsters, preferably from the cold, clear loch-fed waters of western Scotland. If you find that your lobster contains prized coral as you prepare it (look for a dark green sac), save it. This can be mixed into butter to dress fish steaks, or beaten and brushed on large raw prawns prior to frying, to impart a superb flavour and vibrant orangey-pink colour. **SERVES 2 AS A STARTER OR LIGHT DISH**

2 small live lobsters, about 500g
  each
10g sea salt
4 large Charlotte potatoes, about
  100g each
100g wild rocket
100ml Vinaigrette (page 218)
25g piece Parmesan cheese
sea salt and freshly ground black
  pepper

1 First, put the lobsters in the freezer for about 30 minutes to make them sleepy. When ready to cook, make sure you kill them quickly: the simplest way is to detach the head from the body as fast and firmly as possible. Put the lobster, belly-side down, horizontally in front of you on a board. (The claws will be wrapped in thick bands so they won't nip you.) Hold the head firmly with one hand and with your other hand, push the tail hard away from you, then towards you, in two swift moves. This detaches the head from the body quickly. (The two parts may continue to twitch a little because of cut nerve endings, but the lobster is not alive.)

2 Pull the large claws from the head and set aside. Discard the head (or use for lobster bisque, page 12). Clean the body by removing the swim bladder, which is attached to the middle tail section. Holding the body belly-side down, fan out the tail and grasp the middle tail section between your finger and thumb. Bend it upwards, then twist and gently pull to remove the long, thin, opaque tube. Repeat to prepare the other lobster. Tie the tail sections together to obtain perfect medallions (see right).

3 Put a large pan containing at least 3 litres of water on to boil and add the salt. Drop in the lobster bodies and claws, and boil, allowing $3\frac{1}{2}$ minutes for the tails, up to 5 minutes for the claws. Remove and cool a little. Pull the shells from the bodies – it is best to do this while they are still warm. Crack the claws with the back of a heavy cook's knife, then you should be able to pull off the shell in two parts and extract the meat in one piece; set aside.

4 Meanwhile, boil the potatoes in salted water until just tender. Remove and cool a little, then peel them while still warm (wearing rubber gloves to protect your hands from the heat).

5 Blitz half the rocket in a food processor with a little of the vinaigrette, then drizzle in the rest until the dressing is velvety smooth. Taste for seasoning.

6 Slice the potatoes lengthways and arrange in the centre of each serving plate. Spoon over some of the dressing. Cut the lobster tails into medallions and arrange on top. Add the claw meat if liked. Drizzle over more dressing and add the remaining rocket leaves. Using a swivel peeler, pare fine shavings of Parmesan and scatter over the rocket leaves. Serve at once.

PERFECT MEDALLIONS
To obtain neat round medallions, uncurl the lobster tails and press them together, flesh sides inwards, placing them head to tail as shown. Tie securely along the length with kitchen string to ensure the lobster tails keep straight as they cook.

lobster bisque

The gourmet soup of leftovers, this wonderful bisque is light and delicate with an intense shellfish flavour. There's nothing difficult about it …you simply use the heads and shells of lobsters rather than throw them away. Of course, lobster carcasses can be kept in the freezer until you want to make the bisque. Langoustine and crab shells are suitable, too. You'll need a heavy bladed knife or a Chinese chopper to cut up the shells. **SERVES 2–3 AS A STARTER**

shells and heads of 2 lobsters

6 tablespoons olive oil

1 medium onion, finely chopped

2 carrots, finely chopped

1 celery stick or ½ fennel bulb, chopped

1 fat garlic clove, chopped

2 lemon grass stems, chopped

generous pinch of saffron strands (optional)

2 teaspoons Cognac

200ml Noilly Prat, or dry vermouth

1 litre Fish Stock (page 209)

3 plum tomatoes, chopped

1 tablespoon tomato purée

1 large basil sprig

1 large tarragon sprig

1 large parsley sprig

1 bay leaf

100ml double cream

generous pinch of cayenne pepper

sea salt and freshly ground black pepper

1 Chop up the lobster shells and heads, using a large heavy knife or Chinese cleaver – the finer you chop them, the more flavour you will extract. Retain the soft tissue in the heads – this adds to the flavour.

2 Heat half the olive oil in a large saucepan and sauté the lobster shells and heads for about 5 minutes. Remove them with a slotted spoon and set aside.

3 Heat the remaining oil in the pan, then add the vegetables, garlic and lemon grass. Sauté for about 5 minutes until softened. Sprinkle in the saffron if using, and cook for 30 seconds.

4 Deglaze with the Cognac, then add the Noilly Prat and bubble until reduced by half. Return the shells to the pan. Add the stock, tomatoes, tomato purée and herbs. Season with pepper to taste (salt won't be necessary). Bring to the boil, lower the heat and simmer for 20 minutes.

5 Strain the liquor through a large sieve into another pan, pressing the shells with the back of a ladle to extract as much flavour as possible.

6 Bring the strained liquor to the boil and simmer until reduced to about 500ml. Stir in the cream and bring to a gentle simmer. Cook gently for 4–5 minutes. Check the seasoning, adding salt to taste at this stage and cautious pinches of cayenne. Serve hot.

CHEF'S SECRET Noilly Prat is one of my secret flavourings. This classic vermouth with its hint of sweet aniseed is perfect for enhancing fish and shellfish. I often use it in combination with a little Cognac. Like sherry, it is a fortified wine, so once opened it can be kept in the storecupboard.

velouté of jerusalem artichokes with mussels

The French love their terre et mer ('surf and turf') recipes that combine the flavours of the earth and sea, and this one is particularly good. The soup can be made ahead, and the mussels steamed with wine and herbs à la marinière just before serving, then added along with the cooking juices. **SERVES 4 AS A STARTER**

1 Heat the olive oil in a large saucepan and gently sauté the shallots for about 5 minutes until softened but not coloured.

2 Meanwhile, scrub the artichokes under cold water. Add the lemon juice to a bowl of cold water. Slice the artichokes very thinly and immediately add them to the acidulated water.

3 When the shallots are softened, drain the artichokes and add them to the pan. Stir, then cover and sweat for 10 minutes. Add half the wine and cook, uncovered, until reduced by half. Pour in the stock and bring to the boil. Season to taste, lower the heat and simmer for about 15 minutes until the vegetables are soft. Stir in the cream and butter and cook gently for a few minutes, then take off the heat and let cool.

4 Using a slotted spoon, scoop the vegetables into a food processor or blender and whiz until smooth, then gradually add the stock through the feeder tube, with the blades still whirring. Pass the soup through a sieve, rubbing with the back of a ladle. (If preparing ahead, cool and chill until required.)

5 Scrub the mussels well in cold water, discarding any that are open and do not close when tapped. Pull away the beards.

6 Heat a large saucepan until scorching hot. Add the remaining wine, sliced onion and herb sprigs, then tip in the washed mussels. Cover with a tight-fitting lid and cook for about 4 minutes, shaking the pan occasionally, until the mussels have opened.

7 Take off the heat, uncover and leave until the mussels are cool enough to handle. Discard any that have failed to open. Remove the mussels from their shells and set aside. Strain the pan juices into a jug or cup and reserve.

8 To serve, reheat the soup until boiling, stirring in the reserved mussel juices. Divide the shelled mussels between four warmed bowls and pour the soup over them – the heat will be sufficient to warm the mussels through. Serve at once.

3 tablespoons olive oil
2 large shallots, finely chopped
400g Jerusalem artichokes
juice of 1 small lemon
200ml dry white wine
1 litre Chicken Stock (page 210)
150ml double cream
25g butter
500g fresh mussels
1 small onion, sliced
2 parsley sprigs
1 thyme sprig
sea salt and freshly ground black
   pepper

PREPARING JERUSALEM ARTICHOKES Rather than peel this knobbly root vegetable, simply scrub the skins with a small vegetable (or nail) brush. Slice or chop the artichokes, dropping them into a bowl of cold water acidulated with lemon juice as you do so, otherwise they will discolour. Drain before cooking.

mussels with a herb brioche crust

These make a good party canapé, or starter, and you can assemble them an hour or two ahead. Cooked mussels in their half-shell are topped with moist, herby brioche crumbs and gratinéed under a hot grill. I always use freshly cooked mussels, but you do need large ones. If you can only find small fresh mussels, buy about twenty of the New Zealand green-lipped variety instead – these are sold ready cooked in the half-shell. If sweet brioche from a supermarket is the only option for the crumb topping, substitute a rich bread, such as foccacia. **SERVES 4 AS A STARTER**

1kg large fresh mussels
1 shallot, sliced
1 small glass white wine
large knob of butter
sea salt and freshly ground black pepper

Topping:
200g unsweetened brioche, crusts removed
3–4 tablespoons olive oil
1 shallot, finely chopped
1 thyme sprig, leaves only, finely chopped
2–3 coriander sprigs, finely chopped
1 teaspoon finely chopped chives
20g Parmesan cheese, freshly grated

1 Wash the mussels thoroughly, pull away the beards and scrub the shells to remove any barnacles. Discard any mussels that are open and refuse to close when you tap them sharply.

2 Heat a large saucepan until hot, then tip in the mussels, sliced shallot, wine, butter and seasoning. Cover with a tight-fitting lid and cook for about 5 minutes, shaking the pan occasionally. By this time the mussels should have opened; discard any that are still closed.

3 Drain the mussels and leave until cool enough to handle. Remove the mussels from their shells, reserving 20–30 of the largest half-shells.

4 Meanwhile, make the topping. Blitz the brioche in a food processor to fine crumbs, then tip them into a bowl. Heat 1 tablespoon olive oil in a small pan and sauté the shallot for about 3 minutes until softened, without colouring. Add to the crumbs with the chopped herbs and Parmesan. Mix with a fork, adding more oil to moisten as necessary; the crumb mixture should not be dry.

5 Put 2 or 3 mussels in each of the reserved half-shells. Sprinkle the crumb topping over the mussels to cover them completely and press down lightly.

6 When ready to serve, preheat a foil-lined grill pan under a high grill. Lay the mussels on the grill pan and grill for a few minutes until the topping is lightly browned and the mussels are piping hot.

TO CLEAN MUSSELS Mussels that you buy are cultivated in protected areas of the sea bed, or grown on poles fixed in clean sea water. Because of their habitat, they ingest sand and grit as they feed. Live mussels must be bought very fresh. Scrub them clean and remove any barnacles under cold water, using a stiff brush. Then, if time, put the mussels in a large bowl of clean, cold salted water, sprinkle in a handful of oats and set aside for a few hours. The mussels will feed on the oats and expel any grit they contain.

GREEN-LIPPED MUSSELS Use these if you cannot find large fresh mussels. To prepare, wipe the mussels clean. Put them in their half-shells on a baking sheet in a preheated oven at 180°C, Gas 4 for 5 minutes to warm through. Top with the brioche crumb mixture and gratiné under the grill as described in step 6.

salad of marinated oysters with wafer-thin fennel

If the notion of eating raw oysters from the shell doesn't appeal to you, then try them marinated – the best of both worlds. For this salad, shucked oysters are marinated in citrus juices with soy and sesame flavourings, then served on a crisp fennel salad. To serve 4, buy twice as many oysters, but you'll only need to increase the marinade by half as much again. Use a mandolin or Japanese slicer to slice the fennel. **SERVES 2 AS A STARTER OR LIGHT LUNCH**

12 freshly shucked oysters, rock or
   native (see below), juices reserved
1 large fennel bulb
about 100g frisée or wild rocket
1 tablespoon chopped chives
3 tablespoons Vinaigrette (page 218)
sea salt and freshly ground black
   pepper

Marinade:
1 large shallot, finely diced
juice of 2 limes
juice of ½ lemon
1 tablespoon dark soy sauce
1 tablespoon sesame oil
few drops of Tabasco sauce
sea salt and freshly ground black
   pepper

1 Check over the shucked oysters carefully, removing any tiny fragments of shell. Wash them carefully in their reserved juices, then chill.

2 Remove the fronds from the fennel and reserve for garnish. With the tip of a very sharp, small knife, cut out the core from the base of the fennel and discard. Fill a large bowl with cold water and tip in 3 or 4 handfuls of ice cubes. Peel away the outside ribs of the fennel bulb, using a swivel vegetable peeler.

3 Slice the fennel very finely from the cored end using a mandolin, then drop straight into the iced water. Leave the fennel in the iced water for an hour or so; this helps it to become very crisp.

4 In the meantime, mix the marinade ingredients together in a shallow dish. Add the oysters and toss to mix. Leave to marinate for about 15 minutes.

5 Drain the fennel and pat dry with a clean tea towel. To serve, toss the crisp fennel with the frisée or rocket, chives, vinaigrette and seasoning. Divide between plates. Using a slotted spoon or fork, lift the oysters from the marinade and arrange them around the salad. Trickle over a little marinade and garnish with fennel fronds.

TO SHUCK OYSTERS The two main species available in this country are smooth-shelled Natives (or Belons) and the more craggy Pacific rock oysters, which are easier to open. The classic short, stubby oyster knife is the safest implement to use. Make sure the oyster shells are tightly closed; discard any that are not. Take the knife in one hand and protect your other hand with a thick, folded napkin or tea towel. Hold the oyster rounded side down in the cloth or tea towel with the hinge end showing. Keeping the oyster level, slowly but firmly stick the knife point in through the hinge, wiggling it from side to side if necessary, until you feel a 'give' as the hinge muscle is cut. Insert the knife a bit further and twist to lift up the top shell. Tip out the juices into a bowl. Slide the knife under the oyster to cut through the muscle and take out the oyster. Check that it is free of small pieces of shell. Wash the oysters in their own juice then chill.

tempura of oysters

The secret to a light tempura batter is to mix it at the last moment and draw the food to be coated through it lightly. For a light crisp coating, use freshly opened beer and Perrier – one of the fizziest sparkling waters. The batter is ideal for other seafood too, such as large prawns and cubes of monkfish.

Master the art of shucking oysters, following my instructions on the opposite page, and keep the juices – a sublime addition to fish sauces. Alternatively, buy ready shucked oysters from your fishmonger. Serve with the sweet and sour pepper sauce, or a simple dipping sauce of naturally brewed soy sauce with a drizzle of sesame oil. **SERVES 3–4 AS A STARTER**

1 Check the oysters carefully, removing any fragments of shell. Set aside in the fridge until ready to cook.

2 To make the sauce, heat the olive oil in a pan and sauté the shallot and pepper for about 5 minutes until softened but not coloured. Stir in the sugar and seasoning and cook until lightly caramelised. Add the vinegar and cook until reduced right down. Pour in the stock and orange juice and let bubble until reduced by half. Whiz in a blender until smooth then set aside. (If preparing ahead, cool and chill; return to room temperature or reheat gently to serve.)

3 For the batter, sift the flour and cornflour together into a large bowl and add the seasoning. Whisk in the beer and Perrier, using a balloon whisk, until the batter is just smooth.

4 Heat the oil in a deep-fat fryer or deep, heavy-based pan to a temperature of 190°C, or until a cube of white bread dropped in browns in 30 seconds.

5 You will need to deep-fry the oysters a few at a time. Dust them lightly with a little flour to help the batter cling, then draw each oyster quickly through the batter and immediately add to the hot oil. Fry for about 1 minute, then remove with a slotted spoon, drain on kitchen paper and keep warm. Repeat with the remaining oysters, reheating the oil in between as necessary. Finally dust the coriander sprigs lightly with flour and deep-fry in the hot oil for a few seconds until crisp.

6 Serve the oyster tempura at once, garnished with deep-fried coriander and accompanied by the dipping sauce.

12 freshly shucked oysters (see left)
olive or groundnut oil, for deep-frying
3–4 small coriander sprigs, to serve

Batter:
125g plain flour or 'oo' pasta flour,
   plus extra to dust
30g cornflour
½ teaspoon fine sea salt
freshly ground black pepper
150ml light ale or lager
150ml Perrier water

Sweet and sour pepper sauce:
2 tablespoons olive oil
1 large shallot, finely chopped
1 red pepper, cored, seeded and diced
80g soft brown sugar
4 tablespoons sherry vinegar
200ml Chicken Stock (page 210)
100ml orange juice
sea salt and freshly ground black
   pepper

CHEF'S SECRET We always rinse our shucked oysters in their own juices, to remove any fragments of shell that might be sticking to them. The oyster juices have a terrific flavour, so we strain (and sometimes freeze) them to use in soups and sauces.

CHEF'S SECRET We never discard anything that can be used to impart flavour, and that includes scallop corals. The fresh corals are spread on a sheet of baking parchment and dried overnight in a very low oven until they are hard and brittle, then blitzed in a food processor, or ground to a powder. We sprinkle this coral powder over fish dishes, risottos and creamy sauces for pasta. It lends a superb flavour.

salad of truffle dressed scallops

Scallops taste wonderful and can be served in a variety of ways, though they are quite expensive. I use only hand dived king scallops from Scotland which are delivered so fresh they almost pulsate when we prise them open. After cleaning, we wash and dry the scallops then stack them upright in lines in containers and chill overnight to firm up. King scallops are very meaty, so you don't need many per person. **SERVES 4 AS A STARTER OR LIGHT MEAL**

1 Hold the scallop rounded-side down in the palm of your hand and stick the tip of a sharp, strong knife in between the two shells, close to the hinge. Work the knife along the hinge to sever the muscle that holds the shells together. Lift off the top shell, then slip your knife under the nugget of meat with its orange coral and frilly skirt, to ease it away from the shell. Pull away the skirt and remove the black intestinal thread and muscle at the side. Separate the coral from the nugget, wash and dry, then cut each scallop in half horizontally. Chill until ready to cook.

2 Wash and dry the salad leaves, tear into pieces and toss together in a bowl.

3 To make the dressing, put the egg yolk, sherry vinegar, mustard and seasoning into a small mixing bowl and place on a damp cloth to hold it steady. Mix the groundnut and olive oils together in a small jug and gradually whisk into the egg yolk base, a few drops at a time. Keep whisking briskly, and make sure each tiny addition of oil is emulsified before adding more. As the dressing starts to thicken, you can slowly trickle in the oil, whisking all the time. When it is thick, whisk in the truffle oil. Check the seasoning and set aside.

4 Par-boil the potatoes for 5 minutes, then drain and peel while still warm. Leave to cool, then cut into 1cm thick slices. Heat 3 tablespoons olive oil in a frying pan and sauté the potato slices in batches as necessary. Fry in a single layer in the pan for 2–3 minutes on each side until brown and crispy on the outside and cooked through. Keep warm.

5 Dust the scallops lightly with curry powder and season. Heat a heavy-based frying pan or ridged griddle until very hot. Add a thin film of oil, then place the scallops in the pan, in a circle. Cook for 1 minute, then turn (in the same order you placed them in the pan to ensure even cooking). Cook the other side for 30 seconds to 1 minute, until golden. Remove from the pan; rest for 2–3 minutes.

6 Meanwhile toss the salad leaves in a little vinaigrette and season. Cut the truffle, if using, into wafer-thin slices. Arrange the potato slices, scallops and truffle slices in a circle on each serving plate. Place a tall cutter in the centre and fill with the salad leaves, then carefully lift off to leave an impressive tower of salad leaves. (Alternatively, you can simply pile the leaves into the centre.) Beat 3–4 tablespoons of hot water into the truffle dressing to loosen it, and spoon around the salad. Drizzle any remaining dressing over the top and serve.

6–10 king scallops

200g mixed salad leaves (such as frisée, rocket, oak leaf lettuce, lollo bianco)

8 large Charlotte potatoes, about 100g each

olive oil, to fry

a little curry powder, to dust

a little Vinaigrette (page 218)

½ fresh truffle (optional)

sea salt and freshly ground black pepper

Truffle dressing:

1 large free-range egg yolk

1 teaspoon sherry vinegar

½ teaspoon English mustard powder

good pinch of fine sea salt

pinch of freshly ground white pepper

70ml groundnut oil

80ml olive oil

1 teaspoon truffle scented oil

langoustine cocktail

This is my ultimate prawn cocktail! Rather than use the ubiquitous prawn, I buy fresh langoustines, also called Dublin Bay prawns or scampi. These cold water crustaceans are not cheap, but they have the most wonderful sweet flavour. Our supplies are from west Scotland. I poach the langoustines gently in a vegetable nage, then serve them simply with a mayonnaise-style marie-rose sauce on a shredded Cos salad. You can substitute raw tiger prawns for langoustines. **SERVES 4 AS A STARTER**

20 fresh langoustines, size 2
500ml Vegetable Nage (page 211)

Marie-rose sauce:
100ml Mayonnaise (page 219)
2 teaspoons tomato ketchup
1 teaspoon Worcestershire sauce
1 tablespoon Cognac
few drops of Tabasco

Salad:
1 baby Cos or Little Gem lettuce
1 tablespoon finely diced shallot
1 tablespoon diced crisp, sharp apple (Granny Smith)
few basil leaves, finely shredded
1–2 tablespoons Vinaigrette (page 218)
sea salt and freshly ground black pepper

To serve:
pinch of mild curry powder
1 cherry tomato, quartered
½ lemon, peeled and segmented
4 parsley sprigs

1 Bring a large pan of water to the boil. Drop in half of the langoustines and blanch for 30 seconds, then immediately drain and peel (see below). Remove the black intestinal line that runs along the back of each one. Repeat with the remaining langoustines.

2 Bring the vegetable nage to the boil in a pan and lower the heat to a simmer. Drop in the langoustines and poach for 2–3 minutes. Remove the pan from the heat and leave the shellfish to cool in the liquid.

3 Meanwhile, make the sauce. Put the mayonnaise in a bowl and mix in the ketchup, Worcestershire sauce, Cognac and Tabasco to taste.

4 For the salad, roll up the Cos lettuce leaves and shred fairly finely. Put in a bowl with the shallot, apple, basil and vinaigrette, and toss to mix. Season to taste.

5 When ready to serve, remove the langoustines from the nage with a slotted spoon and season lightly. Put a spoonful of sauce in the base of each of 4 cocktail glasses and scatter the salad on top. Arrange the langoustines on the salad, trickle a little sauce over each one and dust very lightly with curry powder. Garnish each cocktail with a cherry tomato quarter, one or two lemon segments and a parsley sprig. Serve at once.

HANDLING LANGOUSTINES Langoustines are sold live in sizes, from 1 to 3. For this recipe I use medium – size 2. They are aggressive creatures and attack each other, so top quality langoustines are often sold in individual tubes to keep them apart. To make them easier to peel, we first blanch the langoustines in boiling water, about ten at a time, for 30 seconds to loosen the shells. As they are easier to shell while still hot, we peel the langoustines as soon as we can handle them.
Pull the head from the body, so the tail meat remains intact, then crack the top of the tail shell with the back of a knife. Push up the meat from the tail end and it should pop out perfectly peeled and in one piece. Save the heads, shells and legs – these are full of flavour and make excellent stock to use for fish soups and sauces. You can always freeze them and make the stock at a later date.

CHEF'S SECRET To check that the white crab meat is free from shell, flake it over a metal tray. If there are any shell fragments you will hear the sound as they fall on the metal.

dressed crab with sauce gribiche

For optimum flavour, if you possibly can, buy live crabs. Otherwise I recommend that you buy freshly cooked crabs from your fishmonger or supermarket fresh fish counter and prepare them yourself (following the illustrated technique overleaf), rather than buy ready dressed crabs. I prefer to flavour the white and dark meat before spooning it back into the shells. Serve with French bread or toasted country-style bread. **SERVES 4 AS A STARTER, OR 2 AS A LIGHT MAIN COURSE**

2 fresh crabs, each 500–600g
  (preferably live)
110g fine fresh breadcrumbs
squeeze of lemon juice
few drops of Tabasco
few drops of Worcestershire sauce
1–2 tablespoons Mayonnaise
  (page 219)
1 teaspoon chopped parsley
1 teaspoon chopped coriander
sea salt and freshly ground pepper

Sauce:
3 free-range eggs, hard-boiled,
  peeled and roughly chopped
1 free-range egg yolk
1 teaspoon Dijon mustard
300ml sunflower or light olive oil
1 tablespoon white wine vinegar
1 teaspoon finely chopped capers
1 teaspoon finely chopped gherkins
½ teaspoon anchovy essence
1 teaspoon chopped parsley
1 teaspoon chopped chervil
1 teaspoon chopped tarragon

To serve:
1 large free-range egg, hard-boiled,
  peeled and halved
2 teaspoons chopped capers
2 teaspoons finely chopped gherkin
1 tablespoon chopped parsley

1 If using live crabs, check the claws are well secured with strong bands. Then lay each crab on its back and, using an awl (or small ice pick), pierce the main nerve centre point behind the eyes repeatedly (from different angles) to kill it. Plunge the crabs into a large pan of boiling water or Court Bouillon (page 208) and boil, allowing about 10 minutes; do not overcook. Remove and cool, then chill (this 'sets' the meat and makes it easier to extract).

2 Meanwhile, make the sauce. Rub the hard-boiled eggs through a sieve into a bowl using the back of a ladle; set aside. Mix the raw egg yolk with the mustard and some seasoning in a bowl. Gradually whisk in the oil, drop by drop to begin with, then in a steady stream (as if you were making a mayonnaise). Stir in all of the remaining ingredients, including the sieved egg. Check the seasoning, cover and chill until ready to serve.

3 Prepare the fresh crabs and extract the meat, keeping the white and brown meat separate (as described overleaf). To prepare the empty shells for serving, remove the thin undershell by cutting along the natural line, using pincers or pliers. Wash the shell thoroughly and dry well.

4 Put the brown meat into a blender with the breadcrumbs, lemon juice, Tabasco and Worcestershire sauce, and whiz very briefly to mix. Season with salt and pepper.

5 Flake the white meat and add the 1–2 tablespoons of mayonnaise, the parsley, coriander and seasoning. Toss with a fork to mix.

6 To serve, rub the egg yolk and white through a sieve with the back of a ladle, keeping them separate. Mix the chopped capers and gherkin together.

7 Spoon the brown crab meat into both sides of the cleaned crab shell, then spoon the white meat into the centre, piling it up well. Garnish with lines of chopped parsley, sieved egg white and yolk (as shown). Put a spoonful of caper and gherkin mixture on each portion of brown meat. Serve at once, with the sauce.

PREPARING A FRESH CRAB Lay

the crab on its back on a clean surface and twist off the large claws.

Hold the shell firmly and push the body section up with your thumbs – it should come out in one piece. Remove the small stomach sac behind the mouth. Pull away the inedible, feathery grey gills ('dead man's fingers') from the body section and discard. Twist off the legs.

Now loosen the creamy brown meat in the main shell with a teaspoon – you should then be able to tip it out easily into a bowl.

Break the large claws with one sharp knock from a mallet and peel away the shell, then ease out the meat in one piece with your thumbs.

Prise out the white meat from the body section and legs, using a pick or skewer.

Keep the firm white meat and soft brown meat separate and check for any stray fragments of shell.

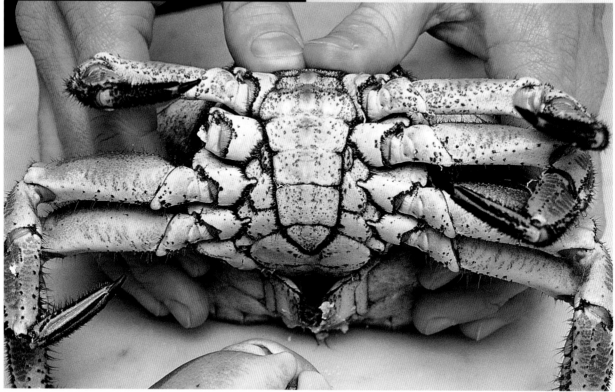

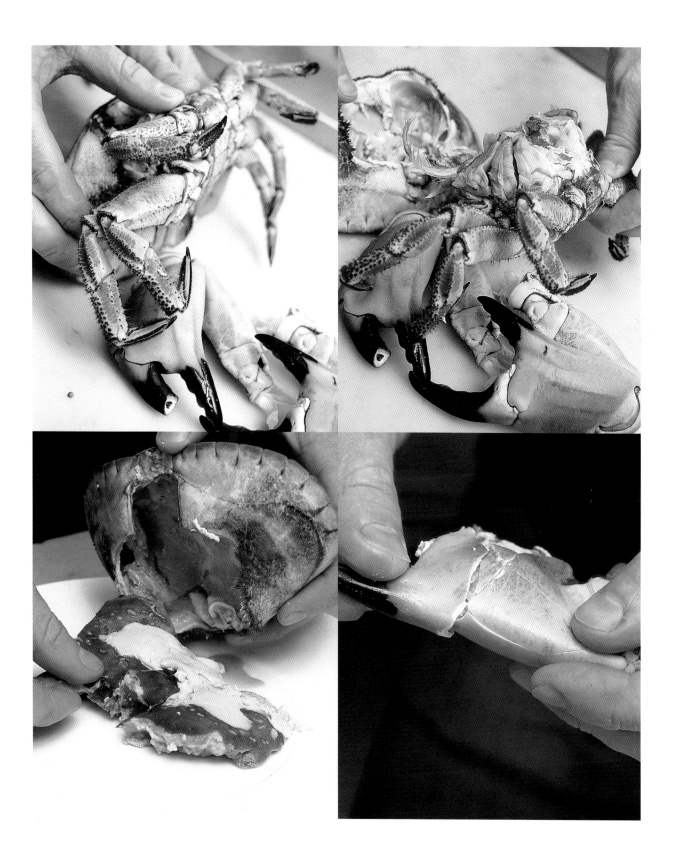

Fish

The fish section was the first I ran as *Chef de partie* in London's Le Gavroche. It was perhaps the busiest section because fish featured as starters and main course. Lackey, the fishmonger delivered the early morning's catch from Brixham around 3.30 each afternoon. The delivery coincided with the end of lunch service and it had to be dealt with pretty quickly. There was little time for a break before starting evening service – all that filleting, trimming and skinning, not to mention handling the wriggling langoustines.

Lackey still delivers to me each day. His blue eyes flashing 'It's up to you now' as he hands over the most perfect specimens you'll ever see. Few chefs survived the fish section without some scars. 'Death Row' we used to call it. But the selection of fish supplied to Gavroche was the best I'd ever seen – small whole turbot, scaly sturgeon, zander, glistening mullets and a terrific variety of fish for the best *bouillabaisse* and *bourride* served in town.

Fish continues to give me the opportunity to re-invent classic dishes in a contemporary way. Simplicity is the essence. Trout are poached in olive oil then crushed with a fork to make rillettes; grilled or fried fish are served simply with a red pepper mayonnaise; while *terre et mer* dishes, such as monkfish wrapped in bacon, combine flavours of the land and sea. Mackerel still remains one of my favourites – juicy and meaty with an almost earthy flavour to team with full flavoured garlic, spices, sharp vinegars and fruits. If we eat more mackerel, our cod stocks might have the chance to revive ...

mackerel and confit potato in aubergine cups

Fresh mackerel is an underrated fish, which is a great shame because it has a good flavour and an excellent texture, and it's not expensive. Of course, you need to choose mackerel that is very fresh – the flesh must feel firm. **SERVES 6 AS A STARTER**

1 large aubergine

olive oil, to drizzle

2 large waxy potatoes, about 300g in total (preferably Desirée or Charlotte)

250g butter, diced

6 large mackerel fillets, about 150g each

juice of 1 lemon

1 tablespoon chopped coriander

1 tablespoon chopped basil

sea salt and freshly ground black pepper

Tapenade:

50g can anchovy fillets, drained

200g pitted black olives

2 tablespoons drained capers

1 fat garlic clove, crushed

1 tablespoon extra virgin olive oil

1 Slice the aubergine lengthways as thinly as possible – a mandolin or Japanese slicer is the best implement to use. Discard the end pieces. Preheat a ridged griddle (or grill) until very hot. Cook the aubergine slices on the griddle in batches for 2–3 minutes, turning to colour both sides. Transfer to a shallow dish and drizzle lightly with olive oil, then brush to coat all over. Set aside to cool.

2 Peel the potatoes, then cut into 1cm thick slices. Melt the butter in a shallow pan over a low heat and continue to heat slowly for 2–3 minutes to about 100°C. Add the potato slices in an even layer and cook gently for about 12 minutes until softened. Remove the potato slices from the butter and drain on kitchen paper.

3 Meanwhile, heat the grill to high. Place the mackerel skin-side down on the grill rack and brush with a little olive oil. Season with salt and pepper and trickle over the lemon juice. Grill for about 5–7 minutes until the flesh feels firm. Set aside to cool, then remove the skin and divide the fish into flakes.

4 Now assemble the moulds. Line two large teacups or similar shaped 200ml moulds with cling film. Line the insides with the aubergine slices, overlapping them slightly and bringing the slices up over the sides (to allow sufficient over-hang to cover the top). Cover the base with a layer of potato slices, press down lightly, season and sprinkle with chopped herbs. Next press a layer of mackerel flakes on top. Repeat these layers twice more, then top with a layer of potato.

5 Fold the overhanging aubergine slices over to cover the top, and press down lightly. Place on a small tray, cover with a board, weight down and refrigerate for a few hours, or preferably overnight. (This helps the layers to set.)

6 Shortly before serving, whiz the tapenade ingredients in a food processor until smooth. Demould the aubergine cups, remove the cling film and place on a board or serving plate. Cut into slices and serve with the tapenade and coarse sea salt.

INDIVIDUAL TIMBALES
Individual sized cups look equally stunning. Use tiny ramekins or similar moulds – no more than 100ml capacity as the starter is quite rich.

CHEF'S SECRET Caramelised aubergine slices give these attractive cups a unique flavour. To intensify their flavour, the wafer-thin aubergine slices are cooked dry (without oil) on a griddle over a high heat until charred and caramelised, then drizzled with olive oil and allowed to cool. The oil imparts flavour and helps to soften the aubergines as they cool. Alternatively, you can create a similar effect by grilling the aubergine slices dry, then using a red hot skewer to mark scorch lines before drizzling with oil.

snapper baked in a salt crust

Oven-roasted fish has a tendency to be rather dry, but this clever Mediterranean baking technique overcomes the problem. The whole fish is encased in salt, which protects it from the intense heat of the oven, seals in the juices and crisps the skin. The result is superb, succulent fish that, surprisingly, doesn't taste salty. Serve the baked red snapper with lemon wedges and a garlicky mayonnaise.

SERVES 2–3 AS A MAIN DISH

1 red snapper, about 800g–1kg, with
   head, fins, tail and scales intact
750g coarse sea salt
handful of thyme or rosemary sprigs

To serve:
flat-leaf parsley
lemon wedges
Garlic Mayonnaise (page 219)

1 Heat the oven to 220°C, Gas 7. Wash the fish and shake to remove excess water, but leave the skin moist.

2 Lay a large sheet of foil in a shallow roasting tin. Spread half the salt on the foil to make a bed, scatter over half of the herb sprigs and place the fish on top. Scatter the remaining herb sprigs over the fish, then pour on the remaining salt to cover the whole fish. Press the salt up against the sides of the fish, then scrunch up the edges of the foil to hold it in place. Don't seal the foil over the top, as steam must be allowed to escape if the skin is to crisp.

3 Bake for 20 minutes, then remove from the oven and leave to stand for 10 minutes. Break off the crisp salt layer, then slide a long palette knife underneath the fish and carefully lift it on to a board.

4 Peel off the skin, which will be easy to remove, and fillet the fish neatly to the bone. Remove the whole skeleton and fillet the fish underneath. The flesh will be moist and juicy. Carefully transfer the filleted fish to a serving platter and garnish with flat-leaf parsley. Serve with lemon wedges and garlic mayonnaise.

BAKING FISH IN A SALT CRUST This is an excellent way to oven-cook whole fish, such as snapper or sea bream. You need a fish with scales intact, and one that has been gutted neatly so the opening can be pinched together to prevent salt seeping inside. The salt forms a brittle coating that is easily broken away after baking, to reveal a perfectly cooked fish.

John Dory with a tomato and cardamom sauce

Curious name for a fish, John Dory. In fact, it has nothing to do with a person, but is an English corruption of the French jaune dorée – meaning golden yellow, the colour of the sheen on the skin when the fish is freshly caught. The flesh is good to eat – creamy white and firm, but not too meaty. Larger fish give better fillets and although it is not a flat fish like sole, it needs to be filleted in the same way. If possible, ask your fishmonger to do this for you.

Here pan-fried John Dory fillets are served with caramelised chicory and a fresh, creamy tomato sauce infused with cardamom. This is a spice with many surprises, not least the way it goes so well with tomato. **SERVES 4 AS A MAIN DISH**

1 Trim the fish fillets to neaten if necessary and set aside.

2 Halve the chicory lengthways and trim the root end, leaving it partly intact to hold the leaves together. Roll the chicory in the sugar until evenly coated.

3 Heat half the olive oil in a shallow pan and fry the chicory on both sides until nicely caramelised. Pour in the stock, season and cook, uncovered, until the chicory feels tender when pressed and the stock has totally reduced, about 20 minutes. Remove and set aside.

4 Meanwhile, make the sauce. Split open the cardamom pods with your finger nails and extract the seeds. Whiz the tomatoes in a blender or food processor with the vinegar, sugar and cardamom seeds. Pass though a sieve into a saucepan, rubbing with the back of a ladle.

5 Bring to the boil and cook for 10 minutes until reduced by half. Pour in the cream and simmer for 2 minutes, then whisk in the butter pieces. Season and set aside; keep warm.

6 Mix the curry powder with 1½ teaspoons fine sea salt and sprinkle over the fish flesh to coat lightly. Heat the remaining oil in a frying pan and fry the fish, skin-side down, for 2–3 minutes. Flip over carefully and cook the other side for no more than 2 minutes.

7 Reheat the chicory, then lay each half on a chopping board and slash lengthways with a sharp knife. Place on the centre of warmed plates and press down lightly to fan out. Lay the fish on top, trickle over any pan juices, then spoon the sauce around.

2 John Dory fillets, each 120g,
  with skin
1 large head of chicory
4–5 tablespoons caster sugar
5 tablespoons olive oil
300ml Fish Stock (page 209) or
  Chicken Stock (page 210)
½ teaspoon mild curry powder
fine sea salt

Sauce:
6 cardamom pods
400g vine-ripened tomatoes, halved
2 teaspoons sherry vinegar
2 teaspoons caster sugar
150ml double cream
50g butter, diced
sea salt and freshly ground black
  pepper

CHEF'S TIP We often season white fish with a curry spiced salt to enhance the flavour. Mixing the curry powder or other powdered spice with salt enables you to apply a light, even sprinkling and avoids 'clumping'.

CHEF'S SECRET To impart a delicate flavour, drizzle a little olive oil on to the red mullet skin, then sprinkle with saffron strands and rub with your fingertips. Leave to infuse for 5 minutes, or so. You'll find the saffron flavour permeates the fish and the skin cooks to a deep golden red colour.

warm salad of saffron red mullet with ratatouille

With its Provençal flavours, this eye-catching dish makes an inviting starter or chic light meal. Red mullet are increasingly on sale here, even in supermarkets. Although we tend to regard them as a Mediterranean species, many are caught in our own seas and sold in prime condition. Buy whole fish and fillet them yourself (following the instructions below), or get your fishmonger or fresh fish counter to do so for you. I like to enhance their attractive red-pink skins with saffron (see below).

SERVES 4 AS A STARTER OR LIGHT MEAL

1 Check the red mullet fillets carefully with your fingertips for pin bones, removing any that you find with tweezers. If the fillets are large, cut each in two crossways. Place the fillets skin-side up on a tray. Mix the saffron strands with 2 tablespoons olive oil and drizzle over the fish. Rub to adhere and set aside to infuse for 5–10 minutes.

2 Meanwhile, heat 2 tablespoons olive oil in a saucepan and gently sauté the chopped red peppers for about 5–7 minutes until softened. Remove and set aside to cool.

3 Whiz half the red peppers in a food processor until smooth and creamy. Add to the mayonnaise and stir until well blended. Set aside.

4 Heat 4 tablespoons of the remaining oil in a frying pan and gently sauté the yellow pepper until softened, about 5 minutes. Add the chopped courgette and aubergine, season and cook for 5–10 minutes until the vegetables are tender.

5 Meanwhile, dip the tomato in a bowl of boiling water for a few seconds, then remove and slip off the skin. Halve, deseed, core and finely chop the tomato flesh. Add to the ratatouille along with the remaining red pepper, and chopped basil. Check the seasoning.

6 When ready to cook, season the red mullet fillets with salt and pepper. Heat the remaining 2 tablespoons oil in a large heavy-based frying pan over a high heat. When the pan is hot, add the fillets, skin-side down, and cook on this side only for about 3 minutes until the skin is really crispy. Take the pan off the heat and leave to rest for 5 minutes. The fish will be three-quarters cooked when you finish pan-frying – it will continue to cook as it rests.

7 Divide the ratatouille between warmed plates and top with the red mullet fillets. Thin the red pepper mayonnaise with a little water if necessary and drizzle a little around each serving. Serve the rest separately.

4 small red mullet about 250g each,
 or 2 larger ones about 500g each,
 filleted (see below)
150ml olive oil, plus extra to drizzle
large pinch of saffron strands
2 red peppers, cored, seeded and
 finely chopped
200g Mayonnaise (page 219)
1 yellow pepper, cored, seeded and
 finely chopped
1 large courgette, finely chopped
1 medium aubergine, finely chopped
1 large plum tomato
1 tablespoon chopped basil
sea salt and freshly ground black
 pepper

TO FILLET RED MULLET

Lay the fish on a board and bend inwards in a slight curve. With a sharp filleting knife, slit the skin from head to tail along the backbone, then cut across just below the head to the backbone. Starting at the head end and keeping the knife flat, skim it across the bones to detach the fillet. Turn the fish over and remove the second fillet in this way. Trim to neaten. If using two larger fish, cut the 4 fillets in half crossways. Don't discard the bones and heads – use to make stock.

trout rillettes in olive oil

Poach fresh, meaty trout fillets in olive oil, then flake and press into ramekins to make a really simple and delicious starter. Serve with crisp, Melba-style sourdough toasts. **SERVES 6 AS A STARTER**

about 500g fresh trout fillets, skinned (see below)

300ml light olive oil

2 tablespoons chopped coriander

2 tablespoons crème fraîche

generous squeeze of lemon juice

sea salt and freshly ground black pepper

sourdough toasts, to serve (see below)

1 Check the trout fillets for pin bones by running your fingertips over the flesh, removing any with tweezers.

2 Heat the olive oil in a medium frying pan over a medium-low heat to a temperature of 100°C; it will take about 2–3 minutes to reach this temperature.

3 Lower in the fish fillets so they are submerged in the oil, then turn the heat to low – the fish should poach not fry. Cook for 4–5 minutes until the trout fillets are lightly coloured on the outside, still pink in the centre, and lightly springy to the touch.

4 Lift the trout fillets from the oil and drain on kitchen paper. Transfer them to a plate and leave until cool enough to handle, then flake using a fork.

5 Tip the flaked trout into a bowl and season with salt and pepper to taste. Add the chopped coriander, crème fraîche and lemon juice to taste. If liked, moisten with a tablespoon or two of the poaching oil. Spoon into ramekins, cover and chill.

6 Serve the trout rillettes with sourdough toasts.

TO SKIN TROUT FILLETS Lay the trout fillet, skin-side down, on a board and make a cut at the tail end so you can lift the fillet slightly from the skin. Grasp the skin with salted fingers and run a sharp medium knife between the flesh and the skin, holding the blade against the skin and the knife at a slight angle, to separate the fillet.

SOURDOUGH TOASTS Preheat oven to 170°C, Gas 3. Cut 6 medium slices of sourdough bread and toast lightly until pale golden brown on both sides. Cut off the crusts then, using a long bread knife, split each slice horizontally in two. Place these thin slices on a baking sheet and bake for about 10 minutes until the bread starts to curl. Cool slightly before serving – the slices will crisp up as they cool. These toasts can be prepared ahead and kept in an airtight container.

pan-fried salmon with bacon and red wine sauce

Salmon is meaty enough to take a smoky bacon and red wine sauce, especially if you accompany it with buttered spinach and a julienne of sweet, young carrots. I serve the fish with its crisp-fried skin uppermost, because it looks so tempting.

SERVES 4 AS A MAIN DISH

1 Trim the salmon fillets to neaten if necessary, then score the skin (see below) and season it with salt and pepper; set aside.

2 To make the sauce, heat a large, wide pan until really hot, then add the olive oil and quickly sauté the lardons for a minute or two until browned. Add the shallots with the garlic and herbs, and cook until softened and caramelised, about 7 minutes. Deglaze with the port, then add the wine and cook until reduced by two thirds. Pour in the two stocks and add pepper to taste. (You won't need salt because the lardons are salty.) Bring to the boil and simmer, uncovered, until reduced by half, about 15–20 minutes. Strain through a sieve, pressing with the back of a ladle. Set aside.

3 For the carrot julienne, cut the carrots into long thin slices, then into very thin sticks. Heat half the butter in a pan and sauté the carrots for a minute or so. Add the 100ml chicken stock or water and a little seasoning. Simmer, uncovered, for about 3 minutes until the liquid is totally reduced and the carrots are glazed. Set aside; keep warm.

4 Heat 2 tablespoons olive oil and the remaining butter in a pan and sauté the spinach for a minute or two, until just wilted. Remove from the heat and season; keep warm.

5 To cook the salmon fillets, heat a non-stick frying pan until hot and add 1–2 tablespoons olive oil. Fry the salmon, skin-side down, for 3 minutes. Flip over and cook the other side for 1–2 minutes. The flesh should be lightly springy when pressed; season lightly.

6 To serve, reheat the sauce. Place a mound of spinach in the centre of each warmed plate and pour over the sauce. Lay a salmon fillet, skin-side up, on top and finish with a little pile of carrot julienne. Drizzle a little olive oil around the sauce if you like and serve immediately.

4 thick-cut salmon fillets, about
  140g each
2 carrots, peeled
50g butter
100ml Chicken Stock (page 210) or
  water
4–5 tablespoons olive oil
about 200g baby spinach leaves
sea salt and freshly ground black
  pepper

Sauce:
3 tablespoons olive oil
100g lardons or diced smoked bacon
1 large or 3 small shallots, finely
  chopped
2 fat garlic cloves, chopped
1 thyme sprig
1 rosemary sprig
1 bay leaf
3 tablespoons port
120ml red wine
400ml Fish Stock (page 209)
500ml Chicken Stock (page 210)

TO SCORE FISH SKIN Use a razor-sharp knife, such as a craft knife or scalpel. Working across the grain of the skin, make shallow cuts just though to the flesh at 5mm intervals, leaving a 1cm border at the edges.

aromatic steamed cod fillets

Thick, juicy cod fillets are steamed over water that is intensely flavoured with a medley of spices, fresh herbs and aromatics. The steam permeates the fish to impart a delicate, lingering flavour that is quite sensational. Naturally, the fish must be very fresh and thickly cut. Firm flesh is a good indicator – flesh that appears to be separating into flakes is beginning to stale. But if you can't find the best cod, then use chunky hake, haddock or sea bass fillets instead. The steaming water can be re-used: simply strain to remove the flavourings, refrigerate and use within a couple of days. **SERVES 4 AS A MAIN DISH**

4 thick-cut cod fillets, about
  175–200g each
1.5 litres water
6 star anise
1 cinnamon stick
10 cardamom pods
10 cloves
1–2 tablespoons pink or Sichuan
  peppercorns
large handful of parsley sprigs
few large thyme sprigs
1 large bay leaf
3 shallots, sliced
½ head garlic
1 vanilla pod, split
1 lemon, cut into 6 slices
about 8 large lettuce leaves, to line
  steamer
few small basil sprigs
few tarragon sprigs
few rosemary sprigs
light olive oil, to drizzle
sea salt and freshly ground black
  pepper

1 Check the cod fillets for any residual bones by running your fingertips over the flesh. If you feel any, pull them out with your fingers or thin pliers. Wrap the fillets tightly in cling film and chill. (If possible, leave them wrapped in the fridge overnight to set the shape.)

2 Put the water into a large pan that will take a large steamer. Add all the spices, parsley, thyme, bay leaf, shallots, garlic, vanilla pod and lemon slices. Bring to the boil, then lower the heat and simmer for 10 minutes. Take off the heat and set aside to infuse for an hour or so.

3 When ready to cook, unwrap the cod. Bring the water and aromatics back to the boil. Line the base of the steamer with lettuce leaves and scatter with the basil, tarragon and rosemary. Place the cod on top and season with salt and pepper. Drizzle with olive oil.

4 Fit the steamer over the pan of simmering water, cover and cook the fish fillets for 4–6 minutes. To test, check that the flesh feels firm when pressed, but take care as steam can easily scald. Lift the fish fillets on to warmed plates. Serve with Whole Spice Basmati Pilaff (page 103) or plain boiled rice, and vegetables of your choice.

salad of seared tuna with a sauté of treviso

I use a portion cut from the tail end of a whole tuna loin for this dish and marinate it overnight. Simply scatter thinly pared strips of orange and lemon zest over the tuna and sprinkle with coarse rock salt, then wrap in cling film and leave in the fridge overnight. This simple technique really improves the texture of this meaty fish. Remember to bring it back to room temperature about half an hour before cooking. Alternatively, you can use ready sliced tuna steaks, as long as they are neatly trimmed and of even thickness. **SERVES 4 AS A MAIN DISH**

4 tuna steaks, preferably freshly cut
   from the loin (tail end), about 120g
   each and 1cm thick
100ml olive oil
2 tablespoons Dijon mustard
1 teaspoon clear honey
2 teaspoons soy sauce
6–8 tablespoons cracked black
   pepper
4 small heads of treviso (red chicory)
   or radicchio
icing sugar, sifted, to dust
1 lemon, quartered

1 If necessary, trim the tuna steaks. Mix half the olive oil with the mustard, honey and soy sauce, and smear all over the steaks. Shake the pepper on to a sheet of greaseproof paper and press the steaks in the pepper until evenly coated.

2 Trim the ends of the treviso and slice in half lengthways. Set aside while you cook the tuna.

3 Heat 1 tablespoon of the remaining olive oil in a large frying pan until very hot and fry the tuna steaks over a high heat for 45 seconds – 1 minute on each side; remove and set aside to rest while you cook the treviso.

4 Preheat a large heavy-based frying pan until almost smoking. Dust the treviso liberally with sifted icing sugar, then drizzle with the remaining olive oil. Place cut-side down in the pan and cook for about 1–1$\frac{1}{2}$ minutes, turning often, until they caramelise on the surface and start to wilt.

5 Divide the treviso between warmed serving plates. Cut each tuna steak in half and place alongside. Squeeze over lemon juice to taste and drizzle over any pan juices to serve.

CARAMELISING BITTER LEAVES This is a great technique for sweetening bitter leaves, to serve as a warm salad. Halve small heads of treviso, radicchio or white chicory lengthways and set aside for 5–10 minutes to allow the bitter juices to exude. Then sprinkle generously with sifted icing sugar and drizzle with olive oil. Sear, cut-side down, in a smoking hot pan, and cook, turning often, until just wilted and caramelised.

pan-fried bream with celeriac velouté

Gilt-headed bream, or dorade, is a versatile fish that can take a delicate or full flavoured sauce. Here it is served with a velouté style sauce, thickened with a purée of celeriac. To add to the earthy feel, I suggest teaming it with girolles and braised celery. **SERVES 4 AS A MAIN DISH**

4 gilt-headed bream fillets, about 120g each

½ small celeriac

90g butter

100ml dry white wine

600ml Fish Stock (page 209) or Chicken Stock (page 210)

100ml double cream

2 small heads celery, about 250g in total

2 tablespoons olive oil, plus extra to cook fish

1 thyme sprig, leaves only

200g girolles (or chanterelles), trimmed

50g baby leaf spinach

sea salt and freshly ground black pepper

PAN FRYING FILLETS
To preserve their delicate texture, 90% of the cooking time should be on the skin side. This helps protect the flesh and gives the skin a crisp texture and inviting colour. To check that it is cooked, press the flesh with the back of a fork. It should feel just firm with a very slight 'give'. Never overcook fish.

1 Trim the fish and check for pin bones, removing any that you find with tweezers or your fingertips. Set aside in the fridge.

2 To make the sauce, peel the celeriac and cut into small dice. Heat 30g butter in a large saucepan and gently sauté the celeriac for about 5 minutes until lightly browned. Add the wine and cook until it evaporates, about 3 minutes. Pour in half the stock and bring to the boil. Cover and simmer gently for 10–15 minutes until the celeriac is soft.

3 With a slotted spoon, transfer the celeriac to a food processor and whiz, gradually adding stock from the pan until you have a smooth sauce. Strain through a fine sieve back into the pan, rubbing with the back of a ladle. Add the cream and bubble gently for 2 minutes. Season and set aside.

4 Meanwhile, cut the celery into thin batons, about 6cm long. Heat a quarter of the remaining butter and 1 tablespoon olive oil in a pan and sauté the celery with the thyme leaves for 5 minutes; don't allow to brown. Pour in the remaining stock and simmer, uncovered, for 10 minutes or until softened. Drain if necessary, and season with salt and pepper.

5 Rinse the girolles quickly in tepid water, drain in a colander and pat dry with kitchen paper. Halve or quarter larger ones. Heat half the remaining butter with 1 tablespoon olive oil in a frying pan. When hot, sauté the girolles over a high heat for about 3 minutes. Season and remove from the pan. Add the remaining butter to the pan and stir-fry the spinach for 1–2 minutes until just wilted. Season and set aside; keep warm.

6 To cook the fish, heat a non-stick frying pan until you can feel a good heat rising, then pour in a thin film of oil. Quickly season the flesh side of the fish and place skin-side down in the pan. Cook for 3–3½ minutes, then turn and cook for 30 seconds or so, until the flesh feels firm. Remove and leave to rest while you reheat the sauce and celery.

7 To serve, divide the spinach between warmed plates and spoon over a little sauce. Place the bream, skin-side up, on top and surround with the celery and girolles. Spoon the hot sauce over the vegetables, leaving the fish skin uncovered. Serve immediately.

sea bass baked on a bed of herbs

This is a really simple recipe, but the flavours are superb. A whole sea bass is cooked on a lavish bed of herbs in a sealed foil package in the oven. Don't fail to savour the full aroma as you open the parcel – it is simply divine. Farmed sea bass is widely available, but I prefer to buy naturally caught fish that has a greater depth of flavour and looks so beautiful. You don't need to include all of the herbs listed below, but use at least four of them. The cooking juices make the accompanying sauce. To serve four, simply buy two fish and cook them in separate foil parcels. (Illustrated overleaf) **SERVES 2 AS A MAIN DISH**

1 Wash the inside of the fish well, making sure the central blood lines are washed away. Trim the tail and fins using scissors, and pat dry, inside and out. Score the skin of the bass on both sides, with the tip of a very sharp knife. Rub the skin with olive oil and season with salt and pepper. Tear off two large sheets of foil, each about 45cm square and set aside.

2 Heat 1 tablespoon oil in a large heavy-based frying pan. Lay the fish in the pan and fry briefly for about 30 seconds on each side to seal and crisp the skin slightly. Remove from the heat.

3 Lay one of the foil squares on a work surface. Scatter the herbs, lemon grass and spices over the centre of the foil sheet and lay the whole sea bass on the leafy herb bed. Drizzle with a little more olive oil and tuck the lemon slices around the fish.

4 Cover the fish loosely with the other square of foil and fold the edges together well to seal. The foil should form a roomy tent around the sea bass, allowing space for steam to surround and cook the fish. Place the foil parcel in a roasting tin and set aside in a cool place to infuse for 1–2 hours until ready to cook.

5 Preheat the oven to 180°C, Gas 4. Put the roasting tin in the centre of the oven and bake for about 20 minutes until the fish is only just cooked.

6 Remove from the oven and leave the fish to rest, still wrapped, for 5–10 minutes before serving. Unwrap the sea bass parcel at the table and spoon the tasty cooking juices over the fish as you serve it.

1 whole sea bass, about 800g–1kg, scaled and gutted
1 tablespoon olive oil, plus extra to drizzle
4 bay leaves
handful of rosemary sprigs
handful of thyme sprigs
handful of tarragon sprigs
handful of basil sprigs
handful of sage sprigs
4–5 lemon grass stems, slit in half lengthways
4 star anise
1 teaspoon mixed peppercorns
1 large lemon, thickly sliced and caramelised (see overleaf)
sea salt and freshly ground black pepper

CHEF'S SECRET Fresh lemon complements fish perfectly, but I prefer to use caramelised lemon slices for this baked sea bass, to impart a more complex and interesting flavour. Simply pan-fry thick lemon slices with a little olive oil for a few minutes until they begin to caramelise around the edges. You will find the lemony flavour is intensified and takes on a different character.

monkfish in Parma ham on creamed Savoy cabbage

Monkfish is now one of, if not the most expensive fish that you can buy. In recent years this superb, meaty fish has become increasingly popular and as demand exceeds supply, so the price rockets. It is the tail that we eat – the huge, bony head is discarded. The central cartilaginous bone that runs the length of the tail is removed to give two fillets. You will also need to remove the outer grey membrane, using a very sharp knife. Here the monkfish fillets are wrapped in Parma ham and served on a bed of creamy cabbage with diced celeriac and carrots. **SERVES 4 AS A MAIN DISH**

1 Using a sharp knife, remove as much of the thin grey membrane that covers the fish as possible. Fillet the monkfish by removing the central bone to give two meaty fillets.

2 Lay the Parma ham slices, slightly overlapping, on a surface lined with a sheet of cling film. Place the two monkfish fillets in the middle, laying them side by side, but head to tail end. Wrap the Parma ham around the monkfish, making sure it is completely covered. Wrap the parcel tightly in cling film. Twist the ends of the cling film to tighten the wrapping and chill for at least 1 hour – this helps set the shape. (You can do this a day in advance.)

3 Peel and dice the carrots and celeriac. Quarter the cabbage and remove the outer leaves. Cut out the core, then shred the cabbage finely. Bring a large pan of salted water to the boil. Have ready a large bowl of iced water.

4 Blanch the carrots and celeriac in boiling salted water for 2 minutes, remove with a slotted spoon and refresh in cold water. Drain and set aside. Blanch the shredded cabbage in the same way, allowing 1 minute. Refresh in iced water, then drain again.

5 When ready to cook the fish, preheat the oven to 180°C, Gas 4 (see right). Remove the cling film from the monkfish parcel, then tie at intervals with string to hold the shape. Heat the olive oil and butter in a frying pan and when it begins to foam, lower in the monkfish parcel and cook, turning frequently, for 3–4 minutes until browned all over.

6 Lift the monkfish parcel into an ovenproof dish, drizzle over the pan juices and roast in the oven for 5–6 minutes until the fish is just firm. Remove from the oven and leave to rest in a warm place for 5 minutes.

7 Meanwhile, pour the cream into a large saucepan, bring to the boil and allow to bubble until reduced by half, then mix into the vegetables. Season to taste and cook for 1–2 minutes.

8 To serve, remove the string from the fish parcel, then cut into 8 thick pieces. Divide the creamy vegetables between warmed serving plates and arrange the Parma-wrapped monkfish on top.

1 monkfish tail, about 600g
about 150g sliced Parma ham
2 large carrots
½ celeriac
1 small Savoy cabbage
about 2 tablespoons olive oil
50g butter
250ml double cream
sea salt and freshly ground black
  pepper

CHEF'S SECRET If you find it more convenient to cook this dish entirely on the hob (and, like me, you are happy to use cling film as a wrapping for steamed food) try the following method – it works brilliantly. Put the wrapped monkfish parcel in a steamer over boiling water, cover and steam for 4–5 minutes. Take out of the steamer and leave to rest for 5 minutes, then remove the cling film. Heat the butter and olive oil in a frying pan until foaming, add the monkfish parcel and pan-fry, turning, for 3–4 minutes until cooked.

Dover sole studded with herb cloutes

I like to cook and serve Dover sole in a simple way to appreciate its fine flavour. For this dish I spike the fish with herb cloutes, cook it briefly on a griddle, then roast the fish in foaming butter. It is best served simply too, with green beans or a salad. If Dover sole is unavailable or too expensive, you can use lemon sole instead. **SERVES 2 AS A MAIN DISH**

2 Dover soles, about 500g each

2 large rosemary sprigs (preferably
   with woody stems)

12 large basil leaves

1 tablespoon olive oil

100g butter, in pieces

2 bay leaves

few thyme sprigs

splash of dry white wine

sea salt and freshly ground black
   pepper

1 Cut away the fins, then remove the dark skin and heads from the sole. Trim the tails. Wash the fish gently and pat dry. Preheat the oven to 180°C, Gas 4.

2 Break the rosemary into smaller sprigs and wrap each sprig tightly in a basil leaf, to make 12 cloutes (see below).

3 Place the sole skinned-side uppermost on a board and insert the stems of the herb cloutes into the fish. Heat the olive oil in a large frying pan or ridged griddle pan and pan-fry the fish for 30 seconds on each side. Meanwhile, heat the butter in a small pan until melted and foaming.

4 Pour the foaming butter into a large baking tin and lay the Dover soles in the tin. Scatter the bay leaves and thyme sprigs on top of the fish and drizzle over the white wine. Season with salt and pepper. Bake for 8–10 minutes, basting the fish once or twice, until the flesh feels firm and flakes easily from the bone.

FLAVOURING FISH WITH HERB CLOUTES

Choose woody rosemary or thyme sprigs and break into smaller sprigs. Slash the stem end of several large basil leaves. Wrap each rosemary or thyme sprig tightly in a basil leaf, starting from the tip of the basil leaf and leaving the woody herb stem protruding. Make small slits in the skin of the fish and insert the cloutes. If the fish is skinned, simply press the woody stems directly into the flesh. The herbs infuse the fish with their flavours during cooking and are easily removed before eating.

TO SKIN DOVER SOLE Lay the fish on a board, dark skin uppermost. Using the tip of a knife, loosen the skin near the tail and grasp it with salted fingers (so you can get a firm grip). Using your other hand to hold down the tail, pull the skin firmly, parallel with the fish, so that it comes away cleanly in one piece. The white skin can be removed in the same way, but if you are cooking the fish whole (as here) you'll find that leaving the white skin on helps keep the fish intact during cooking. (It can be removed easily after cooking.)

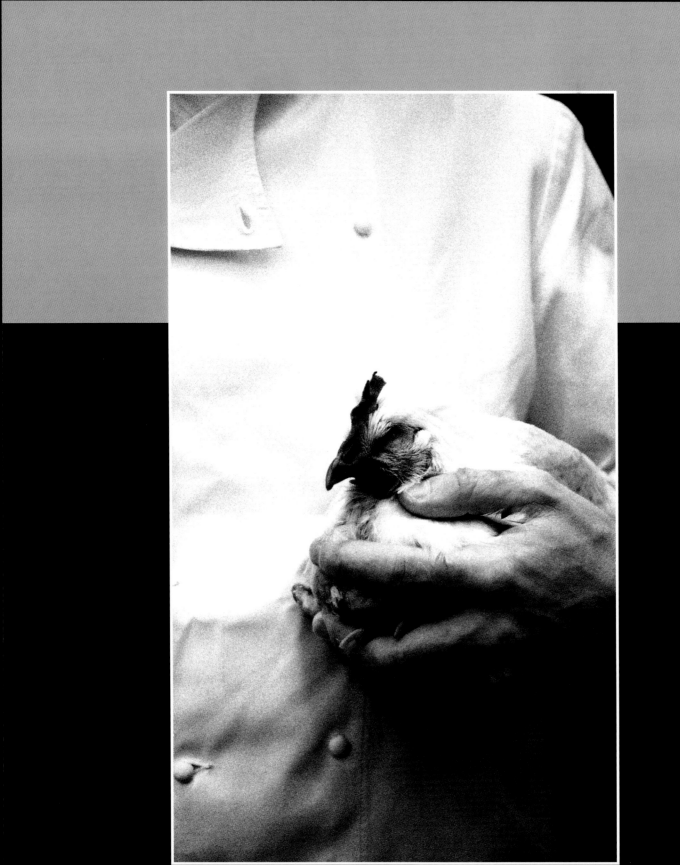

Poultry and game birds

At last, we are beginning to respect the quality of poultry as they do in France. The French really love their poulet de Bresse and rigorously enforce high quality standards. And I am pleased to see that many British birds are now reared in true free-range conditions, giving us meat with a flavour and texture comparable to that of their French cousins. Norfolk-bred black leg chicken and the increasingly popular Gressingham duck are two of my favourites.

We never roast a whole bird because the breast meat will become dry before the legs are cooked. A chef's trick, which ensures both white and brown meat is cooked to perfection, is to separate the legs from the main body. Breasts are roasted on the carcass as a 'crown' moistened liberally with butter to help the skin to caramelise, whilst the legs are cooked separately – often boned and stuffed.

While I love cooking game birds, I hate shooting them. Other chefs may take up the sport and strut around looking macho with a shotgun but I'm a bad shot. I stick to cooking them. Game birds can be a minefield to an inexperienced cook. The secret is to make sure they are well basted during roasting and to watch them carefully, because the meat is so lean and can overcook in seconds. At Le Gavroche, the *Maitre d' hotel* would always carve birds at the table. Timing was critical because the birds needed to rest after roasting, but couldn't be allowed to go cold, as reheating was out of the question. If the '*Maitre D*' came back scowling into the kitchen with the carving knife still in his hand, we knew we were in trouble.

roast chicken with herbs and cardamom carrots

The problem with roasting a large chicken is that the breast and legs take different lengths of time to cook. Remove from the oven when the breast is juicy and tender, and the leg meat is invariably undercooked. Wait until the thigh meat is cooked and the breast will be dry. The trick is to cook them apart. Roast the legs separately to serve with the breast meat, or use for another recipe. Serve the chicken with creamy Pommes Dauphinoise (page 137) for the ultimate Sunday lunch.

SERVES 4–6 AS A MAIN DISH

1 large free-range chicken, about 2kg

200g butter, softened

3 tablespoons chopped parsley

1 large carrot

1 large leek

1 onion

2 celery sticks

½ head of garlic or 5 garlic cloves, peeled

handful of thyme sprigs

few small rosemary sprigs

1 lemon, halved

500g baby carrots, with tops

6 cardamom pods

sea salt and freshly ground black pepper

1 To remove the chicken legs, slash the skin between the thighs and breast, pull the legs right out and dislocate the joints, then cut through and separate the legs from the body; chop off the bony ends.

2 Remove the wishbone to make the breast easy to carve. Lift up the neck skin to expose the wishbone and cut this away from the flesh, using a razor sharp knife. Where the tip meets the breastbone, stick the knife tip in and smash down with your fist to break it for easy removal

3 Preheat the oven to 190°C, Gas 5. Mix half the softened butter with the chopped parsley and season with pepper. Insert the herb butter between the breast skin and flesh (see below). The crown of chicken is now ready to roast.

4 Chop the large carrot, leek, onion and celery and place in a roasting tin. Sit the chicken crown on top. Scatter the garlic cloves and herb sprigs over the surrounding vegetables. Season the chicken skin and place the two lemon halves in the body cavity.

5 Roast for about 30 minutes, basting the chicken with the pan juices 3 or 4 times, to help brown and crisp the skin. (The legs can be roasted separately; allow about 45 minutes.)

6 Meanwhile, trim the carrots, leaving on a little of the green stalks. Melt the remaining butter in a heavy-based frying pan and cook the baby carrots with the cardamom pods and seasoning over a medium heat for about 15 minutes, turning occasionally, until tender and caramelised.

7 When the chicken breast feels firm, check that it is cooked. Insert a thin skewer into the thickest part: if the juices are clear it is done. If they are pink, roast for another 10 minutes or so.

8 Remove the crown roast to a warmed serving dish, cover with a loose 'tent' of foil and leave to rest for a good 15 minutes before carving. The juices will be re-absorbed into the flesh, making it even more succulent. Carve the breast (and legs if roasted at the same time). Serve with the cardamom carrots, and Dauphinoise potatoes if you like.

STUFFING WITH HERB BUTTER To keep the breast moist, spread herb butter under the skin. To do this, work your fingers under the breast skin to loosen it (working from either end), then insert the soft herb butter. Smooth the skin back in position, massaging to spread the butter evenly.

ballottine of chicken with grainy mustard sauce

Flavour is especially important when it comes to chicken – there are too many tasteless birds around as far as I'm concerned. Poulet de Bresse are in a class of their own. I buy these fine-flavoured, plump-breasted black leg chickens from France, but I am increasingly impressed with birds raised by small speciality poultry farmers in this country. For this recipe, look for good, plump free-range chicken suprêmes – boned breast and wing with the small fillet that lies under the breastbone removed. The suprêmes are stuffed with herby sausage meat and poached, then served with a creamy velouté flavoured with grainy mustard. Serve with pasta or Pomme Purée (page 136). **SERVES 4 AS A MAIN DISH**

4 chicken suprêmes, preferably
poulet de Bresse
250g good quality fresh sausage
meat (about 4 thick sausages,
skinned)
1 tablespoon chopped chervil or
parsley
1 tablespoon chopped tarragon
300–400ml Chicken Velouté
(page 212)
1 tablespoon wholegrain mustard
2 tablespoons olive oil
large knob of butter
sea salt and freshly ground black
pepper

1 Remove any sinews from the chicken suprêmes. Using a sharp boning knife, slit each chicken breast horizontally, three quarters of the way through, then open out flat. Season the inside with salt and pepper.

2 Mix the sausage meat with the chopped herbs and spread over the chicken. Roll up tightly and wrap in several turns of cling film, twisting the ends well for a good seal. Chill in the refrigerator for a couple of hours.

3 Bring a large shallow pan of water to the boil. Add the chicken rolls and poach for about 15 minutes until they feel just firm when pressed. Have ready a large bowl of iced water. Slide the chicken rolls into the iced water and leave for 10–15 minutes to cool quickly. Lift out of the water and remove the cling film.

4 Meanwhile, reheat the chicken velouté and stir in the grainy mustard. Taste and adjust the seasoning.

5 Heat the olive oil and butter in a large frying pan. When it starts to foam, add the chicken rolls and fry, turning, for about 5 minutes until nicely browned all over. Leave to stand in a warm place for 5 minutes.

6 To serve, slice the ballottines into rounds and arrange on warmed plates, on a small mound of creamy pomme purée if you like. Pour over the velouté and serve.

VARIATION
Large chicken legs can be stuffed in a similar way. Bone the legs (or ask your butcher to do this), making sure the skin remains intact. Place the sausage meat along the centre, enclose and tie at intervals with kitchen string. Wrap in foil and slow roast at 170ºC, Gas 3 for up to 1 hour until firm and tender, then serve.

poussin with a velouté of navets and white beans

I like to roast these tender, baby chickens, or 'spring chickens', and serve them with an interesting accompaniment. Here baby turnips and haricot beans in a chicken velouté – scented with chervil, chives and truffle oil – fit the bill. You will need to pre-soak the beans and prepare some velouté in advance. This is a really nice winter dish. **SERVES 4 AS A MAIN DISH**

1 Soak the dried beans in cold water overnight, then drain and place in a saucepan. Add plenty of cold water to cover, bring to the boil, and add the onion, carrot and bay leaf. Simmer for 1 hour or until just tender. Drain, refresh under cold running water and drain again, discarding the flavourings. Season and set aside. Preheat the oven to 190°C, Gas 5.

2 Blanch the baby turnips in boiling water for a minute or so, then drain and refresh under cold running water. Peel the turnips thinly, cut into quarters and season with salt and pepper.

3 Brush the poussins with the melted butter and season. Cover the breast of each with a butter paper or a small piece of foil. Roast for about 20–25 minutes until cooked. To check the poussins, pierce between the leg and breast: if pink juices run out, allow an extra 5–10 minutes in the oven.

4 Meanwhile, put the haricot beans and baby turnips into a saucepan with the velouté and bring to the boil. Simmer, uncovered, for 10 minutes or so, until the sauce is reduced by one third. Check the seasoning and stir in the chopped herbs and truffle oil.

5 When the poussins are cooked, rest in a warm place for 10 minutes before serving. Strain off the pan juices into a small saucepan, heat until bubbling, then whisk in the vinaigrette.

6 You can serve the birds whole or jointed if you prefer (see below). Divide the velouté of turnips and white beans between warmed serving plates. Sit the poussin on top and drizzle over the vinaigrette sauce to serve.

125g dried haricot beans
1 small onion, sliced
1 small carrot, halved
1 bay leaf
16 baby turnips (navets)
4 poussins, 400–500g each
about 40g butter, melted
300ml Chicken Velouté (page 212)
1 tablespoon chopped chervil
1 tablespoon chopped chives
few drops of truffle oil
100ml Vinaigrette (page 218)
sea salt and freshly ground black
  pepper

CHEF'S SECRET Poussins are often served whole, but I prefer to cut them up to make life easier for my guests. Using a sharp knife, cut through the thigh joint and remove the legs. We then pull out the thigh bone, leaving the drumstick in place, but you don't have to do this. Carefully cut the breasts from the bone in one piece and discard the carcasses. Arrange the whole poussin breasts and legs on the plates.

Claridges chicken pie

A great favourite on the menu at Claridges, enjoyed by many of my guests. We bake the filling and pastry separately so the chicken remains succulent, and the pastry is light and crisp. You can either serve individual pies ready plated as we do, or a whole one in a traditional pie dish (see below). **SERVES 4 AS A MAIN DISH**

1 Cut the chicken into 2cm chunks. Dip the onions in boiling water for 30 seconds to loosen the skins, then remove and peel. Bring the stock to the boil in a shallow pan, add the onions and cook for 5 minutes. Lift out with a slotted spoon.

2 Add the chicken, bay leaf and thyme to the stock. Return to a gentle simmer and poach for 5 minutes, then take off the heat and leave to cool in the liquid for a minute or two. Strain the stock into a jug, discard the herbs and season the chicken lightly; set aside.

3 Cut the pancetta into lardons (2cm strips). Heat a quarter of the butter in a frying pan or wok and stir-fry the pancetta until crispy, about 3 minutes. Remove and drain on kitchen paper. Wipe out the pan.

4 Melt the remaining butter in the pan. When it starts to foam, add the mushrooms and stir-fry for about 7 minutes until softened, seasoning to taste.

5 Pour in the sherry and bubble until well reduced. Return the bacon and onions to the pan and pour in the reserved stock. Bring to the boil and cook until reduced by half. Add the cream and bubble until reduced by a third. Add the chopped herbs and set aside.

6 Heat the oven to 200ºC, Gas 6. Roll out the pastry on a lightly floured surface to the thickness of a £1 coin. Cut out four rounds, using a small saucer as a template. Carefully place the pastry rounds on a large non-stick baking sheet and score the surface in a diamond pattern, using the tip of a small sharp knife.

7 Brush the pastry with the egg yolk glaze and bake for about 10 minutes until risen and golden. Bake for a further 2 minutes with the oven door slightly ajar, to help crisp the pastry. Remove from the oven and slide on to a wire rack.

8 Meanwhile, add the mushrooms to the sauce and reheat until bubbling, then add the chicken. As soon as the chicken is warmed through, check the seasoning and divide between warmed serving plates. Top with a pastry round and serve.

4 skinless, boneless chicken breasts, about 120g each
125g baby onions
500ml Chicken Stock (page 210)
1 bay leaf
1 thyme sprig
200g pancetta or good smoked bacon, in one piece
100g butter
250g shemigi mushrooms, or baby button mushrooms
100ml dry sherry
200ml double cream
2 teaspoons chopped tarragon
1 tablespoon chopped parsley
250g Puff Pastry (page 190)
1 egg yolk, beaten with 1 teaspoon water
sea salt and freshly ground black pepper

TO SERVE AS A TRADITIONAL PIE Prepare the filling as above. Cut out one large pastry lid, using the inverted pie dish as a template and place on a baking sheet. Cut the pastry lid into quarters and move them apart slightly, then score, glaze and bake as above. Tip the filling into the pie dish and assemble the pie lid on top to serve.

poché-grillé quail with a honey mustard dressing

Oven-ready quails are now available from most good supermarkets, as well as butchers and poulterers. Allow two per person for a main course, one each for a starter. Most of the meat is on the breasts. Cooking quail on a griddle or barbecue can dry the delicate flesh, so I apply a poached-grilled technique (see overleaf). Thereafter, I toss them with a spiced honey dressing and serve on a bed of sauté potatoes with a rocket salad. **SERVES 4 AS A MAIN DISH**

8 oven-ready quails

1 litre Chicken Stock (page 210)

handful of thyme sprigs

8 small rosemary sprigs

finely pared zest of 2 limes, in strips

a little olive oil, to brush

sea salt and freshly ground black
  pepper

Dressing:

6 tablespoons clear honey

1 tablespoon soy sauce

1 tablespoon coarse grain mustard

1 tablespoon Dijon mustard

1 tablespoon sesame oil

1 Un-truss the birds to loosen them up, then re-truss by securing them with wooden cocktail sticks or simply tying the legs together at the tips with string.

2 Put the chicken stock in a medium saucepan, add the thyme sprigs and bring to the boil. Add the quails, return to a simmer and cook for 2 minutes, then remove and drain upside down in a colander. You may have to do this in two batches.

3 Pat the birds thoroughly dry with kitchen paper. Stuff the cavity of each quail with a rosemary sprig and a few lime zest strips.

4 Whisk the dressing ingredients together in a jug and set aside.

5 Heat a ridged griddle (or barbecue) until you can feel a steady medium high heat – not too high or you will char the flesh. Lightly oil the griddle.

6 Brush the quails lightly with a little olive oil and season lightly. Cook on the griddle (or barbecue) for about 7–10 minutes, turning several times with tongs, until the birds are golden brown all over and the breasts are firm. Be careful not to burn the delicate flesh.

7 Transfer the quails to a warmed, large shallow bowl and pour over the dressing. Leave to marinate for 5 minutes, or a little longer. Untie the legs and remove the rosemary and lime zest from the cavities. Serve the quails on a bed of sliced sautéed potatoes with a rocket salad.

CHEF'S TIP The stock will have taken on extra flavour from the quails, so don't discard it. Cool and use again – perfect for a velouté.

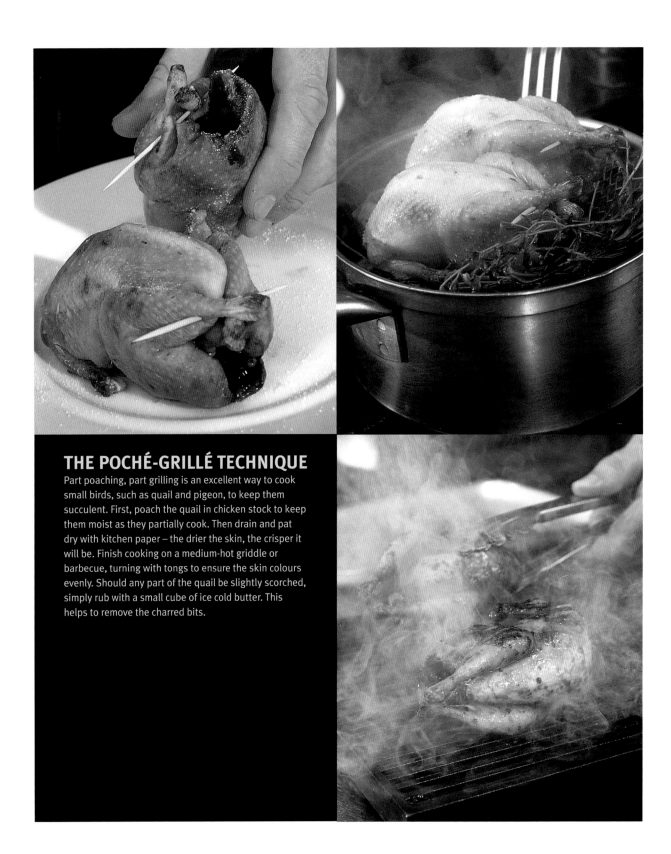

THE POCHÉ-GRILLÉ TECHNIQUE

Part poaching, part grilling is an excellent way to cook small birds, such as quail and pigeon, to keep them succulent. First, poach the quail in chicken stock to keep them moist as they partially cook. Then drain and pat dry with kitchen paper – the drier the skin, the crisper it will be. Finish cooking on a medium-hot griddle or barbecue, turning with tongs to ensure the skin colours evenly. Should any part of the quail be slightly scorched, simply rub with a small cube of ice cold butter. This helps to remove the charred bits.

duck 'bresaola'

Skinned duck breasts are dry-cured in a spiced salt over a period of 4 days, then cut into wafer-thin slices, carpaccio-style, for an easy and impressive starter. Use very fresh, prime quality meat – either one large Barbary duck breast, or 2 smaller ones from a Gressingham duck. Both have a mild gamey flavour that suits marinating. Serve with chicory leaves, or a leafy salad dressed with walnut vinaigrette. **SERVES 4–6 AS A STARTER**

1 large Barbary duck breast, about
   400g, or 2 smaller Gressingham
   duck breasts, about 225g each
20–30g coarse sea salt
¼ teaspoon black peppercorns
4 star anise, broken up
¼ teaspoon coriander seeds
grated zest of 1 orange
grated zest of 1 lemon
olive oil, to drizzle

1 Turn the fridge to its lowest setting, 2–3°C maximum. Remove the fat from the duck breasts and trim away any sinews, then place the trimmed breasts in a shallow dish.

2 Grind the salt, peppercorns, star anise pieces and coriander together, using a pestle and mortar or an electric spice grinder. Mix in the grated orange and lemon zests.

3 Spread the spiced salt mixture on top of the duck breasts to cover evenly and press down. Cover with cling film and place in the fridge for 24 hours.

4 Uncover, turn the duck breasts and rub the spiced salt into the other side. By now, some salty liquid will have started to exude as the breasts begin to shrink. Cover with cling film again and return to the fridge for 24 hours.

5 After the 48 hours, remove the breasts and rinse in cold water. Pat dry, then wrap each breast in clean muslin (not cling film). Place on a plate and refrigerate for another 48 hours to mature.

6 After this, remove the duck breasts from the muslin and open-freeze on a tray for an hour to firm. Now, take a razor sharp carving knife and slice off wafer-thin slices at a slant in a D-shape, as you would cut a side of smoked salmon. Arrange the duck slices in a circle on chilled serving plates and cover with cling film until ready to serve.

7 Drizzle a little olive oil over the duck slices and serve with a salad.

spiced roasted duck legs with a sweet sour sauce

Duck breasts may be the most popular cut of this rich poultry bird, but I recommend that you try slow roasting the legs. These also have a layer of fat under the skin, which bastes the meat during cooking to keep it moist. I use Gressingham ducks, a breed derived from mallard with a semi-gamey flavour. Duck legs are widely available, sold separately and relatively inexpensive. Here they are roasted with aromatic spices and served with a Spanish style citrus and sherry vinegar sauce.

SERVES 4 AS A MAIN DISH

1 Stab the skin of the duck legs a few times with a fine skewer. Mix all the spices together and rub into the legs. Place the duck in a dish and leave to marinate in the fridge for about 2 hours.

2 Preheat the oven to 180°C, Gas 4. Place the duck legs, skin-side up, in a roasting tin and roast for 45–50 minutes. There is no need to baste them during roasting, simply turn once or twice and roast undisturbed to allow the skin to become really crispy. Pour off the fat halfway through cooking. (Keep this for roasting potatoes.)

3 When the ducks are very tender, transfer to a warmed plate and leave to rest, uncovered, in a warm place. For the sauce, sprinkle the sugar into the meat juices in the roasting tin and add the honey. Cook on the hob, stirring with a wooden spoon, until nicely caramelised.

4 Deglaze with the sherry vinegar and allow to bubble until reduced by half. Stir in the orange and lemon juices and bubble again until reduced by half. Strain the sauce through a fine sieve into a bowl and beat in a knob of butter. Season with salt and pepper to taste.

5 Serve the duck legs with the sweet sour sauce. Crispy sautéed potatoes and a watercress salad are good accompaniments.

4 duck legs (preferably Gressingham)
1 teaspoon ground coriander
1 teaspoon ground mace
1 teaspoon ground ginger

Sweet sour sauce:
25g sugar
2 tablespoons clear honey
150ml sherry vinegar
juice of 2 oranges
juice of 2 lemons
pan juices from the roasted duck legs
large knob of butter
sea salt and freshly ground black
  pepper

breast of guinea fowl with pomegranate dressing

Pomegranates are popular in Middle Eastern cooking, and the juice is often used in meat and game dishes. Here it is reduced to concentrate the flavour, then combined with vinaigrette, more pomegranate seeds, pink grapefruit and walnuts, to make an original, fragrant dressing for full flavoured guinea fowl. You could also serve quail or pheasant breasts in the same way.

SERVES 4 AS A MAIN DISH

3 ripe pomegranates

1 pink grapefruit

3 tablespoons cranberry juice

3 tablespoons freshly squeezed
orange juice

6 tablespoons Vinaigrette, made
with half olive oil, half walnut oil
(page 218)

2 tablespoons freshly chopped
walnuts

4 guinea fowl breasts, about 125g
each

a little olive oil, for cooking

sea salt and freshly ground black
pepper

1 Halve the pomegranates and carefully scoop out the seeds, discarding the membrane. Cut the peel and pith from the grapefruit, then cut out the segments using a small, sharp knife. Roughly chop the grapefruit flesh, reserving the juice.

2 Blitz two thirds of the pomegranate seeds in a blender with the cranberry, orange and reserved grapefruit juices, then pass through a sieve placed over a small pan, pressing with the back of a spoon. Boil to reduce by about half, until slightly syrupy, then add to the vinaigrette.

3 Pick over the remaining pomegranate seeds, removing any stray membrane, then add to the dressing with the grapefruit segments and walnuts; set aside.

4 Trim the guinea fowl breasts to neaten and rub the skin with olive oil and seasoning. Heat a heavy-based non-stick frying pan, then fry the breasts, skin-side down, for about 3 minutes. Turn the breasts over and cook the other side for 1–2 minutes. Do not overcook the meat – it should be very slightly pink.

5 Slice each guinea fowl breast horizontally into three. Arrange on warmed plates spooning the pomegranate dressing in between. Serve with wilted spinach and Whole Spice Basmati Pilaff (page 103) or sautéed potatoes.

PREPARING POMEGRANATES Look for these reddish-yellow hard-skinned fruits in markets and shops from September through to December. Use at the peak of ripeness, when the juice is at its sweetest. To prepare, halve vertically, then carefully spoon out the fleshy seeds. It is important to remove all of the creamy yellow membrane, which is very bitter.

pigeon breasts sous-viede with port and Madeira

The sous-viede technique (described below) is a brilliant way of cooking pigeons to retain all their natural flavour and juices. We enrich these juices with a date and orange purée to make a delicious sweet-sour sauce – you'll need to make the purée in advance (see below). The pigeon breasts are best served slightly pink, on small mounds of buttered spinach or blanched shredded cabbage, surrounded by roasted root vegetables such as carrots and baby parsnips. **SERVES 4 AS A MAIN DISH**

4 wood pigeons

1 small onion, sliced

1 carrot, chopped

1 celery stick, chopped

1 bouquet garni (bay leaf, few parsley
   stalks, thyme sprig)

1 star anise

4 juniper berries

2 tablespoons port

2 tablespoons Madeira

small handful of thyme sprigs

2 bay leaves

sea salt and fresh ground black
   pepper

2 tablespoons date and orange purée
   (see below)

THE SOUS-VIEDE TECHNIQUE We often apply this in the restaurant kitchen. Small heatproof plastic pouches are filled with meat or vegetables, a small amount of stock or wine is added with herbs and seasonings, then the bags are vacuum-sealed and placed in pans of simmering water. The food inside cooks in its own juices and the result is a pure simple flavour that is quite superb. Buy 'multi-purpose cooking bags' and you can do something similar at home.

1 First prepare the pigeons. Cut off the legs and most of the backs – these snap easily about halfway along; reserve the legs and bones. Trim the sides to neat 'crowns' of breast and wing joints, cover and place in the fridge.

2 Put the pigeon legs, bones and trimmings in a large pan with the onion, carrot, celery, bouquet garni, star anise and juniper berries. Add about 600ml cold water to cover and bring to the boil. Lower the heat and simmer, uncovered, for about 45 minutes until reduced right down to a quarter of the original volume. Strain the stock into a jug.

3 When ready to cook, bring a large pan of water to boil. Place the pigeon crowns in two 'multi-purpose cooking bags'. Divide the port, Madeira and stock between them, and add the herbs and seasoning. Press out as much air as possible and seal the bags by knotting the open end, as close to the food as possible.

4 Drop the bags into the boiling water, return to a gentle simmer and cook for 10 minutes for pink meat, shaking the bags twice to baste the pigeon in the juice. If you prefer pigeon cooked longer, allow an extra 2–3 minutes at this stage.

5 Lift out the bags (leaving the water simmering) and rest for 2 minutes, then shake to distribute the contents, return to the pan and cook for another 2 minutes.

6 Take out the bags and cut open. Strain the juices through a sieve into a small pan, add the 2 tablespoons date and orange purée and heat until bubbling. Meanwhile, rest the pigeons for 5 minutes.

7 Using a very sharp thin bladed knife, cut away the pigeon breasts in one piece; they should be cooked lightly pink. Arrange on warmed plates, on mounds of spinach or cabbage if you like, and spoon over the sauce. Surround with roasted root vegetables, or serve with Celeriac Lasagne (page 129) if you prefer.

DATE AND ORANGE PURÉE

We use this purée to enrich many game sauces. Put 125g chopped stoned dates, 100ml fresh orange juice and ½ cinnamon stick in a pan and simmer for about 10–12 minutes until the dates have softened. Discard the cinnamon stick. Whiz the dates and juice in a blender until smooth. Spoon into a clean jar and keep in the fridge for up to 1 month, or freeze.

roast grouse with juniper and red wine sauce

The Glorious Twelfth (of August) marks the start of the grouse season, which lasts until December 10th. It means more to sportsmen than chefs, because ideally game birds should be allowed to hang before cooking. I won't even consider putting grouse on my menus until the end of August. The red grouse in Scotland feed almost entirely on heather, which gives their flesh a unique, aromatic flavour.

Many gourmets would say grouse is an acquired taste. Along with teal and partridge, this game bird needs careful handling but, cooked properly, it can be delicious. The meat is very dark and lean, with a strong aroma, and should only ever be cooked pink. Because it has very little fat, grouse must be 'barded' with fat before roasting, to prevent it becoming dry. A brace of grouse will serve two, but you can easily double up the quantities to serve four. **SERVES 2 AS A MAIN DISH**

1 Preheat the oven to 200°C, Gas 6. Take out the hearts and livers from the grouse cavities and reserve for the game croûtes (see below). Lay strips of pork fat over the breasts.

2 Heat half the olive oil in a large heavy-based frying pan and brown the birds all over, pressing them on to the hot pan to seal and colour.

3 Transfer the grouse to a roasting dish, standing them upright if possible, and season with salt and pepper. Roast for 7–10 minutes, depending on size, basting once or twice with hot butter. Remove from the oven and leave to stand in a warm place for about 5 minutes.

4 Using a sharp, thin bladed knife, remove the whole breasts from the birds; they should be nice and pink inside. Set aside on butter papers or greaseproof paper. Chop up the legs and carcasses, return to the roasting dish and roast for a further 15 minutes.

5 Meanwhile, heat the rest of the olive oil in a large saucepan, add the onion and other chopped vegetables and cook until softened and nicely caramelised, about 10 minutes. Add the roasted legs and carcasses, plus the juniper berries and red wine. Cook until the wine has reduced right down, then pour in the stock. Bring to the boil and simmer until reduced by two thirds. Strain the sauce through a sieve into a jug and check the seasoning.

6 To reheat the grouse breasts, place cut-side down on the butter papers and return to the oven for about 3 minutes to heat through; don't let them overcook, they must be pink. Cut each breast into 3 slices. Serve on warmed plates with the sauce, buttery Savoy cabbage, sauté potatoes and the game croûtes. Accompany with old-fashioned bread sauce.

2 oven-ready grouse

thin strips of pork fat or streaky bacon, to bard

3 tablespoons olive oil

50g butter, melted and hot

1 small onion, chopped

handful of chopped vegetables (such as carrots, turnips, celery)

6 juniper berries

200ml red wine

500ml Brown Chicken Stock (page 210)

sea salt and freshly ground black pepper

GAME CROÛTES

Chop the grouse hearts and livers and fry in about 25g butter with a few thyme leaves for about 5 minutes. Deglaze with a splash of red wine, season to taste, then whiz to a paste in a blender or food processor. Fry neat, crustless triangles of sliced white bread in some butter until golden brown and crisp, then drain on kitchen paper. Spread the croûtes with the grouse liver paste to serve.

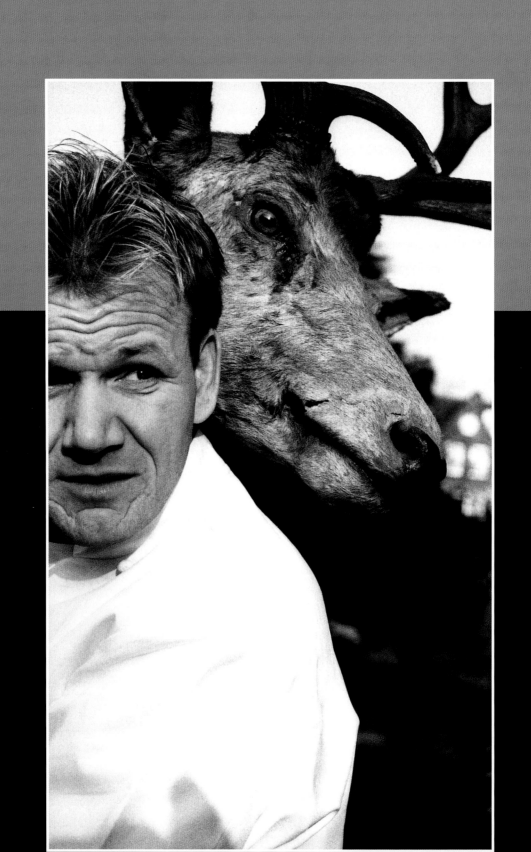

Meat

When I reflected on my choice of recipes for this chapter, I realised just how many of my dishes are moving towards the rustic. I love the challenge of taking so called 'poor' cuts and turning them into superlative meals. Belly of pork, shin of beef and lamb shanks can be transformed into dishes fit for a new rich man. And, of course, we have a generation of new young diners who have been brought up on quick cook cuts of meat, many of whom have never had the opportunity to enjoy country-style dishes.

Slow roast pork and lamb faggots are a revelation – full of flavour, fork-tender and presented in a way that rivals many great haute cuisine classics. I won't pretend these are quick to prepare but they are certainly not difficult to cook if you follow the recipes and techniques I give in this chapter.

Naturally, I appreciate the finer top cuts and look to ways to cook – and serve – them to perfection. Take meltingly tender fillet steaks and succulent calves liver, for example. Here, I pan-sear fillet steaks ahead and top them with a gratin of mushrooms ready to finish cooking in a hot oven to serve. Yes, it is possible to do this and serve the meat piping hot and rare. As for calves' liver, forget slicing it thinly to flash fry, let alone dusting it with flour – the sure way to end up with hard leathery liver. Instead, cut it the thickness of a rump steak and cook until pink and juicy, to serve alongside grilled polenta.

braised belly of pork in a rich glaze

This spectacular dish regularly appears on my menus. Belly pork may be a cheaper cut, but it responds beautifully to slow, gentle cooking – becoming meltingly tender. You may need to order this cut in advance from your butcher – persuade him to prepare it for you too, if you can. I like to serve this with truffle scented Pomme Purée (page 136), lightly wilted spinach and steamed asparagus spears. **SERVES 4 AS A MAIN DISH**

1 whole pork belly joint, about 1kg

4 tablespoons olive oil

1 carrot, chopped

1 onion, chopped

1 leek, chopped

1 celery stick, chopped

½ head garlic or 6 fat garlic cloves, peeled

100ml sherry vinegar

200ml soy sauce

1.5 litres Brown Chicken Stock (page 210)

5 star anise

20 coriander seeds

10 white peppercorns

10 black peppercorns

1 To prepare the pork, use a sharp filleting knife to cut off the skin, leaving a thin layer of fat about 5mm thick. Remove the rib bones and discard. Even out the thickness by taking a slice from any thicker areas and placing where the meat is thinner. You should now have an even sheet of boned pork belly. Roll this up quite firmly and tie into a neat, even-shaped roll (see overleaf).

2 Heat a shallow flameproof cast-iron casserole or deep sauté pan (with lid) until you feel a strong heat rising. Add 2 tablespoons olive oil and brown the pork joint, turning until caramelised all over. Remove to a plate.

3 Add the remaining olive oil to the pan and sauté the vegetables and garlic for about 5 minutes. Deglaze with the sherry vinegar and cook until reduced by half, then return the pork joint to the pan, placing it on top of the vegetables.

4 Pour in the soy sauce and stock, then add the whole spices. Bring to the boil and partially cover the pan. Braise slowly over a low heat, or in the oven at 170°C, Gas 3. Cook for 2½–3 hours, basting occasionally with the pan juices, until the meat feels very tender. To test, push a metal skewer into the middle of the joint; there should be little resistance.

5 Lift out the meat and set aside to rest on a warmed plate. Strain the pan juices into a pan and bubble to reduce to a glossy brown glaze.

6 To serve, remove the string and cut the pork roll into portions, or thick slices. Arrange on warmed plates and surround with wilted spinach and asparagus. Serve with pomme purée.

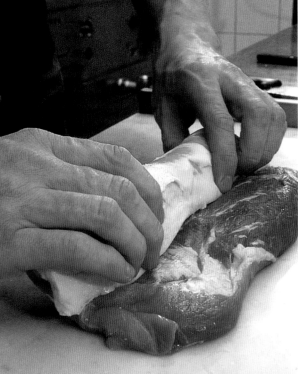

TO TIE A ROLLED JOINT First, cut a long piece of kitchen string and tie the joint lengthways, leaving at least 10cm on one end of the string. Then tie a piece of string around one end of the roll and knot firmly. Next, cut a long piece of string and tie to one end of the knot you have just made. Pull it along 3–4cm and loop around the meat, pulling the string through once but not knotting. Repeat by pulling and looping at 3–4cm intervals until you reach the end of the roll. Tie the string to the loose end (from the first tying).

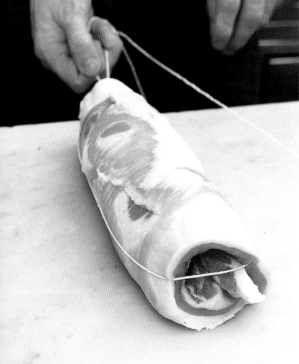

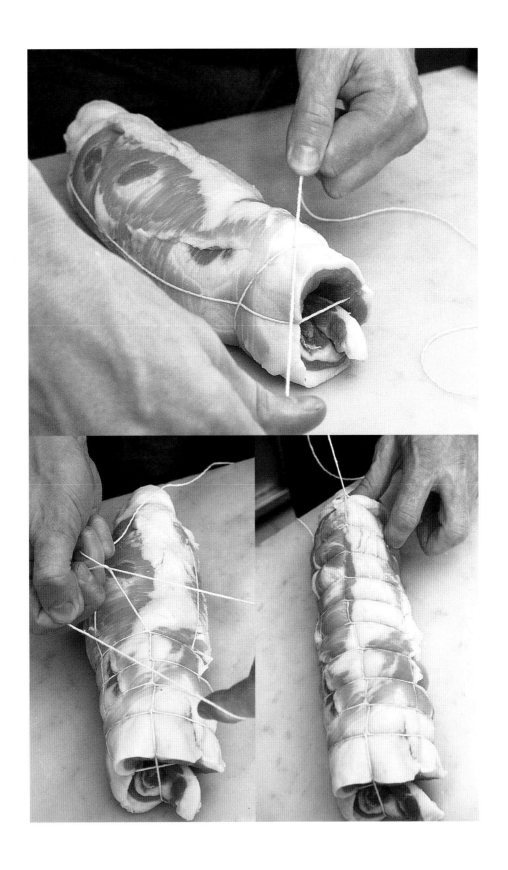

beef fillet with a gratin of wild mushrooms

This is a great way of cooking thick juicy beef fillet steaks. You do need prime quality, thick cut steaks from a neat, round whole fillet, which can only come from a quality butcher who cuts to order. For convenience, the steaks can be seared and topped with the mushrooms in advance, ready to finish in a hot oven just before serving. Ideal if you are entertaining.

SERVES 4 AS A MAIN DISH

1 Prepare the topping ahead. Gently sauté the shallot and garlic in 1 tablespoon olive oil for about 5 minutes until nicely softened.

2 Add a further 2 tablespoons olive oil and sauté the mushrooms over a high heat, stirring frequently, for about 7 minutes until browned and cooked. Add the wine and cook until it has reduced away. The mixture should be quite dry. If necessary, tip it into a sieve to drain off any remaining liquid. Transfer the mushrooms to a bowl, season and mix in the herbs. Allow to cool.

3 Whip the cream until softly stiff, then fold into the mushrooms along with the egg yolk. Cover and chill.

4 Brush the steaks with the remaining tablespoon of olive oil and season them. Heat a large non-stick frying pan until you can feel a strong heat rising. Cook the steaks for about 2–3 minutes, turning them to sear all over. Remove from the pan, season and allow to cool.

5 When ready to serve, heat the oven to 220°C, Gas 7. Put the steaks on a shallow baking tray. Pile the mushroom mixture on top of the steaks and dust with Parmesan. Cook, uncovered, for about 5–7 minutes until the topping is bubbling and golden. Serve as soon as possible, with roasted or sautéed potatoes and a salad.

1 shallot, finely chopped

1 fat garlic clove, crushed

4 tablespoons olive oil

100g wild mushrooms (such as ceps, girolles, blewits, morels), trimmed and finely chopped

100g chestnut mushrooms, chopped

2 tablespoons white wine

1 tablespoon each finely chopped parsley, chervil and chives

4 tablespoons double cream

1 large egg yolk

4 fillet steaks, about 180g each and 4cm high

2 tablespoons freshly grated Parmesan cheese

sea salt and freshly ground black pepper

CHEF'S SECRET For this dish, we buy a whole fillet of beef, weighing approximately 600g. To prepare, we trim the ends and cut away any sinews, then wrap the whole fillet tightly in cling film and chill it overnight. This helps to set the shape, to give you perfectly round steaks.

butter-roasted fillet of beef with baby artichokes

For a very special roast, I buy a whole fillet of beef and cook it simply in foaming butter. Serve with sautéed artichoke hearts and a creamy horseradish-flavoured Pomme Purée (page 136). Trickle the irresistible buttery juices over the beef slices and you won't need to make a sauce. **SERVES 4 AS A MAIN DISH**

1 whole, thick fillet of beef, about
  600g
16 baby globe artichokes, or 4 large
  ones
5 tablespoons olive oil
70g lightly salted butter, cut into
  small cubes
sea salt and freshly ground black
  pepper

1 Check that the membrane has been removed from the fillet. This is visible as a silvery film – use a razor sharp filleting knife to remove it if necessary. Wrap the beef fillet tightly in cling film, rolling it a few times and twisting the ends tightly to seal. Chill for at least 4 hours, preferably overnight, to help set the shape.

2 Meanwhile, prepare and cook the artichokes as for Fondant of Globe Artichokes (page 124). If using large artichokes, cut the hearts into quarters. Set aside.

3 When ready to cook, unwrap the beef and season. Preheat the oven to 180°C, Gas 4. Use a sauté pan that you can put into the oven. (If you do not have a suitable pan, put a small roasting tin in the oven to heat).

4 Heat the sauté pan (or a frying pan) until you can feel a good heat rising. Add 2 tablespoons olive oil and brown the beef fillet, turning it until evenly caramelised. This should take about 5 minutes.

5 Add the butter gradually and allow to foam, then spoon over the meat. Place the pan in the oven (or transfer the beef to the hot roasting tin and pour over the butter). Roast the fillet for 20 minutes, spooning over the butter at least twice in that time. Press the fillet with the back of a fork: it should feel lightly springy. If it feels quite soft, baste well and give it another 5 minutes in the oven.

6 Transfer the beef to a warmed plate, reserving the pan juices, and rest in a warm place for 5 minutes while you finish the artichokes. Heat the remaining olive oil in a frying pan and sauté the artichokes until golden brown and crisp on the outside. Season and remove from the heat.

7 Strain the buttery pan juices from the meat through a fine sieve and reheat. Cut the beef into eight even slices and place two on each warmed dinner plate, adding any juices from carving to the pan juices. Surround the beef with the artichokes and drizzle over the juices. Serve with horseradish pomme purée.

CHEF'S SECRET We clarify butter for many uses, but not when the dish calls for foaming butter. The milky solids (or impurities) in the butter encourage it to foam, so the last thing you want to do is remove them.

A CUT ABOVE THE REST For melting tenderness, you cannot surpass a good fillet of beef. I strongly recommend that you buy from a quality butcher, rather than a supermarket. Flavour is all important, so make sure the fillet is from an animal that has hung for a good 3 weeks, preferably Aberdeen Angus.

leg of lamb with a mushroom and spinach stuffing

This is perfect for a special Sunday lunch and easy to prepare – especially if you get your butcher to bone out the lamb for you. You'll need a medium leg boned out flat (rather than tunnel-boned). Use the bones to make stock and reduce to concentrate the flavour – the basis for a delicious gravy. Serve with potatoes roasted in goose fat and flageolet beans tossed in a little butter and parsley. **SERVES 6 AS A MAIN DISH**

1 Bone the lamb so that it opens out flat (or get your butcher to do so) and spread it on a board, skin-side down. Using a sharp knife, cut out any sinews or excess fat and trim away 150g flesh. Put this through a food processor and whiz to a purée. Add the cream, $\frac{1}{2}$ teaspoon salt and some pepper and blend briefly until smooth. Turn into a bowl, cover and refrigerate, with the boned joint.

2 Chop the mushrooms as finely as possible. Heat the butter in a frying pan and sauté the shallot or onion and garlic for about 3 minutes until softened. Add the mushrooms and fry, stirring, over a high heat until softened and browned, about 7 minutes. Season well, then allow to cool.

3 Blanch the spinach in boiling water for 1 minute, then drain and plunge into a bowl of ice-cold water to refresh. Drain thoroughly, squeeze dry, then chop finely and mix with the mushrooms and tarragon. The mixture should be quite dry. If necessary, wrap in clean muslin and squeeze out any liquid. Add the spinach and mushrooms to the lamb purée, mix well and check the seasoning (see Chef's Tip).

4 Lay the lamb flat on a work surface and spread the stuffing evenly over the inside, then roll up firmly and tie at intervals with kitchen string to secure. If necessary, sew any open edges together with a trussing needle and thread. Roll the neat stuffed joint tightly in cling film and refrigerate for a couple of hours to help set the shape.

5 Preheat the oven to 180°C, Gas 4. Unwrap the meat and weigh to calculate the cooking time. Allow 50 minutes per kg for medium rare meat and 55 minutes per kg for medium. Add 12 minutes for each additional 250g. Place the joint in a roasting tin, drizzle with a little olive oil and sprinkle with seasoning. Lay a butter paper on top to prevent over-browning. Roast the lamb for the calculated time – around $1\frac{3}{4}$–2 hours, basting every 30 minutes with the meat juices.

6 Transfer the meat to a platter and rest in a warm place for 15 minutes or so. Strain the juices into a small saucepan, add the stock, wine and rosemary and bubble for a few minutes to reduce down, then strain into a jug. Carve the meat into fairly thick slices, tipping any juices that seep out into the jug. Serve the meat with the gravy.

1 leg of lamb, about 2.3–2.5kg

2 tablespoons double cream

250g mushrooms, wild or cultivated (or a mixture of both), trimmed and cleaned

70g butter

1 shallot, or $\frac{1}{2}$ onion, finely chopped

1 fat garlic clove, chopped

250g baby leaf spinach

1 tablespoon chopped tarragon

a little olive oil, to drizzle

300ml well-flavoured reduced lamb stock

150ml red wine

few rosemary sprigs

sea salt and freshly ground black pepper

CHEF'S TIP Tasting a stuffing that contains raw meat to check the seasoning is never a good idea, yet it's important to get this right. I fry off a teaspoonful of the stuffing in a little oil until just firm, then taste it and adjust the stuffing seasoning accordingly.

lamb shank faggots in lettuce

Lamb shanks are braised slowly to give very tender meat, which is then shredded and enriched with some of the braising liquid and flavourings, then pressed into balls, wrapped in blanched lettuce leaves and poached. An impressive and unusual main course, best served on a creamy parsnip purée with roasted root vegetables, and steamed asparagus and baby leeks.

SERVES 8 AS A MAIN DISH

olive oil, to fry

4 large lamb shanks

1 carrot, roughly chopped

1 onion, roughly chopped

1 leek, roughly chopped

1 celery stick, roughly chopped

½ head garlic, or 6 fat garlic cloves

1 thyme sprig

1 bay leaf

1 rosemary sprig

2 star anise

4 cardamom pods

8 black olives

300ml dry white wine

1.5 litres Brown Chicken Stock
  (page 210)

18 outer Baby Gem lettuce leaves
  (from about 4 lettuce)

sea salt and freshly ground black
  pepper

To steam:

2 bay leaves

2 thyme sprigs

1 teaspoon coriander seeds

1 Heat a large frying pan until you can feel a strong heat rising, then add a little olive oil and brown the shanks all over, turning frequently. Remove and set aside.

2 Heat a little more olive oil in the pan, add the chopped vegetables and garlic, and sauté for 5 minutes to soften. Add the herbs, whole spices and 4 olives. Pour in the wine and boil until reduced right down to a thin syrup.

3 Transfer the vegetable mixture to a large cast-iron casserole or heavy-based saucepan with a tight-fitting lid and place the lamb shanks on top. Pour in the stock and bring to a simmer. Season, cover and cook at a very gentle simmer for 2½–3 hours until the meat is very tender. Leave in the liquid for 30 minutes, then transfer to a dish with a slotted spoon and cool completely. Strain the liquid into a shallow pan, discarding the vegetables and flavourings, then boil rapidly until reduced to a rich glaze, about 350ml; set aside.

4 Pick the meat from the bones and snip off any sinews. Now pull the meat into fine shreds with your fingertips and place in a bowl; you should have around 500g. Chop the rest of the olives and add to the lamb with 200ml of the glaze. Mix well and check the seasoning, then chill. Reserve the remaining glaze.

5 When ready to shape the faggots, blanch the lettuce leaves, a few at a time, in a large pan of boiling water for about 5 seconds until wilted. Lift out with a slotted spoon and refresh in a bowl of ice-cold water. Remove, drain and pat dry with kitchen paper.

6 Divide the meat into 8 portions. Roll neatly into balls but don't press too firmly. Lightly oil a medium ladle and line with 3 blanched leaves, overlapping the leaf tips in the centre and allowing the stem ends to overhang the edge. Place a lamb ball in the middle and fold over the overhanging leaves pressing lightly to mould. Repeat with the remaining balls and lettuce leaves to make 8 'faggots'. Chill on a plate, join-side down.

7 When ready to serve, add the bay leaves, thyme and coriander seeds to a large pan of boiling water. Place a butter paper on the base of a bamboo steamer (that fits the pan) and place the wrapped lamb balls on top. Position on the steamer pan, cover and cook for about 12 minutes until piping hot. In the meantime, reheat the remaining glaze. Serve the lamb 'faggots' on a bed of creamy parsnip purée, surrounded with vegetables, and drizzled with the glaze.

blanquette of lamb

A blanquette is a classic technique of cooking meat by poaching in stock until tender, then enriching the broth with an egg and cream 'liaison'. Traditionally a blanquette has a very thin sauce, but you can thicken it slightly with a small knob of beurre manié if you like (see below). Stewing veal is generally used for a blanquette, but lean lamb neck fillet works well and is much easier to find. Serve with plain boiled rice or tagliatelle. **SERVES 4 AS A MAIN DISH**

600g lamb neck fillet

300ml Chicken Stock (page 210)

150ml dry white wine

1 bouquet garni (bay leaf, thyme
  sprig, parsley stalks)

1 carrot, cut in small dice

250g baby shallots or button onions

250g button mushrooms, cleaned
  and quartered

4 free-range egg yolks

150ml double cream

squeeze of lemon juice

2 tablespoons chopped parsley

sea salt and freshly ground black
  pepper

1 Trim any excess fat from the lamb, then cut into 2cm cubes. The meat will have a marbling of fat, which helps to keep it succulent.

2 Place the lamb in a saucepan, season and cover with cold water. Bring slowly to the boil and skim off any scum that rises to the top, with a large metal spoon. Simmer for 10 minutes, skimming frequently until there is nothing left to skim. Drain the lamb in a colander and rinse in cold water.

3 Return the lamb to the clean pan and add the stock, white wine, bouquet garni and carrot dice. Bring to the boil, lower the heat and simmer very gently, uncovered, for about 30 minutes.

4 Meanwhile, immerse the shallots or button onions in a pan of boiling water for 30 seconds to loosen the skins, then drain and peel. Add the onions to the lamb and continue to simmer for about 10 minutes. Add the mushrooms and cook for another 5 minutes.

5 By now the meat should be nice and tender. Strain the liquid into a shallow pan. Set aside the lamb, onions and mushrooms, discarding the bouquet garni. Simmer the stock until reduced by a third.

6 Beat the egg yolks and cream together in a small bowl. Remove the pan of stock from the heat and slowly pour a little on to the yolks and cream, whisking as you do so. Pour this liquid back into the remaining stock. Return the pan to the lowest heat possible and stir slowly with the whisk, until it starts to thicken. Do not let it boil or it will curdle. The sauce is ready when it coats the back of a spoon thinly (like a thin custard).

7 Return the lamb and vegetables to the sauce and reheat very gently, without boiling. Tip into a warmed serving dish. Check the seasoning and add a squeeze of lemon juice to taste. Scatter with the chopped parsley and serve.

BEURRE MANIÉ This is used to thicken a sauce, such as a blanquette, if required. It can be made in advance – in quantity if you like – and kept in the fridge to have to hand whenever you want to thicken a liquid quickly. Melt 15g butter in a small pan, mix in 1 tablespoon flour and cook, stirring, for 30 seconds or so. Whisk into the liquid in tiny pieces and cook until thickened. For a blanquette, add the beurre manié to the liquid before you add the egg yolks and cream.

rabbit in pancetta with barley and kidney risotto

Farm reared rabbit is a light, lean and tender meat that is easy to prepare and cook. Traditionally whole rabbits are sold with their kidneys still attached, which can be chopped and stirred into this country-style barley risotto. If you buy leg joints (without kidneys) from your butcher or supermarket, use lamb's kidneys instead. **SERVES 4 AS A MAIN DISH**

1 Using a small sharp knife, remove the thigh bones only from the legs. Wrap each part-boned leg in pancetta or Parma ham to make neat rolls. Pierce each leg in three places and insert the rosemary sprigs pushing them well into the flesh. Refrigerate for about an hour to help set the shape.

2 Put the pearl barley, carrot, onion, leek, celery, thyme sprig, bay leaf and stock into a large pan. Bring to the boil, stirring occasionally. Add seasoning and simmer, uncovered, for about 20 minutes until the grains are soft. Pick out the vegetables and drain the barley, reserving the stock. Set the barley aside while you cook the rabbit and kidneys.

3 Preheat the oven to 190°C, Gas 5. Halve the kidneys and snip out the cores, then chop into small dice. Heat half the olive oil in a small frying pan and sauté the kidneys until nicely coloured and just firm, about 3–4 minutes; do not overcook. Season and remove from the heat.

4 Heat the remaining olive oil in an ovenproof sauté pan and seal the rabbit legs all over. Transfer to the oven and roast for about 20 minutes, turning the legs halfway through cooking. To check that the meat is cooked, insert a thin metal skewer; it should meet with little resistance and the juices should run clear. If not, return to the oven for an extra 5–10 minutes. Allow to stand in the warm pan while you finish the risotto.

5 Put the barley into a saucepan with the reserved stock and stir over a medium heat until piping hot. Stir in the butter so the pearl barley grains become glossy. Off the heat, add the kidneys and chopped parsley. Check the seasoning.

6 Divide the risotto between warmed serving plates. Cut each rabbit leg into 3 or 4 pieces and place on the barley. Place the sauté pan on the hob and pour in the vinaigrette. Heat gently, stirring well to incorporate the meat juices, then spoon over the rabbit. Serve garnished with small parsley or thyme sprigs.

4 rabbit legs (including thighs)

150g thinly sliced pancetta or 100g Parma ham

12 tiny rosemary sprigs

250g pearl barley

1 carrot, quartered

1 onion, quartered

1 leek, halved

1 celery stick, halved

1 thyme sprig

1 bay leaf

1 litre Chicken Stock (page 210)

4 rabbit kidneys or 2 lamb's kidneys

about 4 tablespoons olive oil

70g butter, in pieces

2 tablespoons chopped parsley

6 tablespoons Vinaigrette (page 218)

sea salt and freshly ground black pepper

4 small flat-leaf parsley or thyme sprigs, to garnish

CHEF'S TIP Rabbit is a lean and tender meat that is best protected during roasting to prevent it becoming dry. Wrapping the meat in pancetta or bacon is an effective way to keep it moist.

CHEF'S SECRET To retain its silky texture and delicate flavour, cook calf's liver as you would a fillet steak, rather than in thin slices which overcook in mere seconds. Allow the liver to rest for 5 minutes after cooking, to firm up before serving.

calf's liver with fried polenta and fig vinaigrette

Calf's liver has a fine, delicate texture that is easily toughened if you cook it in thin slices – the best way to ruin it in my view. I prefer to pan-fry thicker 'steaks' which get a better 'cuisson' and so retain their sweet succulence to delicious effect. Ask your butcher to cut you a thick piece of liver and portion it at home. Crisp-fried wedges of polenta are the perfect accompaniment. And to continue the Italian theme, I make a dressing with crushed fresh figs. Mouth-wateringly good!

SERVES 4 AS A MAIN DISH

1 First, make the polenta. Put the milk, water, olive oil, thyme and 1 teaspoon salt into a large, deep pan and bring to the boil. Trickle in the polenta as you stir briskly with a long handled spoon. Always stir in one direction to avoid lumps forming. The mixture will thicken fairly quickly and start to splutter a bit. Don't be tempted to cover the pan as you need to stir the mixture. Cook the polenta for 15–20 minutes over a low heat, stirring frequently.

2 Remove from the heat and stir in the butter and Parmesan, then tip the polenta into a shallow tray and spread to a depth of about 1.5cm. Leave until cool and set, about 1 hour, then cut into wedges. Allow 2–3 wedges per serving. (Wrap any that you don't need now in cling film, refrigerate and use within 3 days.)

3 To make the dressing, break open two of the figs and scrape out the flesh into a bowl, breaking it up with a fork. Gradually mix in the vinaigrette, then set aside.

4 Trim the liver of any tubes or membrane, then cut into 4 even portions. Cut the remaining 4 figs in half lengthways. Set aside while you cook the polenta wedges.

5 Dust each polenta wedge with seasoned flour. Heat a 5mm depth of olive oil in a large frying pan. When hot, fry the polenta for about 2 minutes on each side until golden brown. Remove and drain on kitchen paper; keep warm. Wipe out the pan.

6 Heat 3 tablespoons olive oil with the butter in the frying pan. Dust the liver with seasoned flour, then add to the hot pan. Fry for 2–3 minutes on each side depending on thickness, until the liver is browned on the outside, but still nicely pink and juicy inside. To check whether it is ready, press the surface with your fingertips: if it feels lightly springy it's ready. If the liver feels very bouncy, it will be undercooked. Allow to rest for 5 minutes before serving.

7 At the same time, cook the fig halves. Fry these, cut-side down, in a lightly oiled pan (or alongside the liver if there is room) for about 2 minutes without turning.

8 Place the liver on warmed plates and sprinkle with a little balsamic vinegar. Arrange the fried polenta wedges alongside and top with the hot figs. Pour the fig dressing into the pan, stirring to combine with the meat juices, then drizzle around the liver and serve.

6 fresh figs
100ml Vinaigrette (page 218)
400g calf's liver in one thick slice, 4–5cm thick
flour, to dust
olive oil, to fry
25g butter
aged balsamic vinegar, to serve
sea salt and freshly ground black pepper

Polenta:
600ml milk
600ml water
2 tablespoons olive oil
1 teaspoon thyme leaves
1 teaspoon salt
250g polenta grains (not the quick-cook variety)
30g butter
30g Parmesan cheese, freshly grated

BALSAMIC VINEGAR

A few drops of balsamic vinegar provide a sharp contrast to rich meat dishes, such as meltingly soft calf's liver. Always use a brand that has been aged by the traditional method – in wooden casks for at least 10 years. Dark in colour, aged balsamic vinegar has a wonderful mellow flavour.

navarin of venison with roasted root vegetables

A navarin is normally a slow-cooked casserole of lamb with potatoes and onions. My version uses lean venison which I sauté and serve with a selection of winter roots, brown butter Brussels sprouts and a beautiful shallot and raspberry vinegar red wine sauce. You could call it a posh stew. Parsnip crisps are the ideal accompaniment. **SERVES 4 AS A MAIN DISH**

600g loin of venison

2 carrots

½ celeriac, about 300g

150g baby Brussels sprouts, trimmed

50g butter

6 tablespoons olive oil

sea salt and freshly ground black
   pepper

Sauce:

2 tablespoons olive oil

8 small or 2 large shallots, sliced

1 thyme sprig

1 bay leaf

1 fat garlic clove, sliced

75cl bottle red wine

2 tablespoons raspberry vinegar

800ml Brown Chicken Stock
   (page 210)

To serve:

Parsnip Crisps (page 134)

1 First, make the sauce. Heat the olive oil in a large saucepan, add the shallots and sauté for about 10 minutes until softened and lightly browned. Add the thyme, bay leaf and garlic, sauté for a minute or two, then pour in the wine and 1 tablespoon of the vinegar. Bring to the boil, then boil rapidly until reduced to about 100ml of rich glaze.

2 Pour in the stock, return to the boil and cook over a medium heat for about 20 minutes. Pass through a sieve and return the liquid to the pan. Boil this down to about 200ml, skimming frequently to remove any scum. You should have a wonderful shiny sauce that is thick enough to lightly coat the back of a spoon. Stir in the remaining raspberry vinegar and check the seasoning. Set aside.

3 Cut the venison into 4cm cubes. Peel the carrots and celeriac and cut into 2cm dice. Boil the sprouts for just 2 minutes, then drain and plunge into a bowl of iced cold water or run them under cold water in a colander.

4 Heat the butter until it begins to foam. Watch carefully and as soon as the butter stops foaming and has turned a light brown colour, pour the liquid into a cup, leaving the solid particles behind. Set the liquid butter aside.

5 Heat 3 tablespoons olive oil in a pan and sauté the diced vegetables for about 10 minutes, stirring occasionally, until just tender. Season and remove to an ovenproof plate. Keep warm, uncovered, in a low oven.

6 Wipe out the pan, then add the remaining olive oil and place over a medium high heat. Sauté the venison cubes until caramelised on all sides, but still pink in the centre, about 7–10 minutes. Season well. The venison chunks are ready if they feel lightly springy when pressed. Keep warm while you finish the sprouts.

7 Reheat the clarified nut brown butter in a sauté pan. Add the sprouts and toss well to coat in the butter and heat through.

8 Reheat the sauce. Divide the meat and vegetables between shallow serving bowls and pour over the sauce. Serve at once, scattered with parsnip crisps.

Pasta and rice

I first honed my pasta-making skills under Marco Pierre White in the heady days of Harveys Restaurant, Wandsworth. Marco is one amazing teacher and I was an entranced follower. He taught me the meaning of fingertip control and the discipline of flexible fingers as I moulded hundreds of perfect raviolis each week. I even found myself going through the motions with my hands in the early morning cab back to my small flat. I had to make sure the fillings were moulded into perfectly rounded flying saucer shapes.

Cooked fillings called for thin pasta, raw fillings like lobster needed to be wrapped in thicker pasta. There was a pasta machine designated for each. I messed up once and put a fresh lobster filling in the wrong pasta. The lot went in the bin and the cost, £45, was deducted from my wages. It was a hard lesson, but one I never forgot. Fresh pasta dough is made twice a day in all my restaurants and features in practically every course – including starters, main courses and even sweet petit fours.

It was in the Paris kitchens of Guy Savoy where I learnt the secret of blanching risotto grains and finishing off a risotto of shellfish with mascarpone and white truffles. I remember my time there well. As a new British commis with precious little French under my belt, I found that my inability to speak the language gave me certain advantages. For a start I couldn't understand the oaths hurled in my direction but I also learnt to keep my head down and learn, learn, learn – everything from turning an artichoke to washing and drying spinach.

homemade pasta

Rolling homemade pasta is really a job for two people – one to crank the machine and one to tease the sheet of pasta out of the rollers and stop it folding back on itself – though of course it's possible to manage by yourself if there isn't anyone around to help. This basic recipe produces quite a large amount of pasta dough, because I find it easier to make a larger quantity than work with a small amount. For tagliatelle, ravioli and tortellini, you will need about half of this quantity. You can freeze the pasta sheets that you don't need straightaway in batches for later use. Interleave them with freezer tissue wrap and seal well, or keep well wrapped in the fridge for a few days. Italian 'oo' pasta flour (doppio zero) is now widely available from delicatessens and good supermarkets. **MAKES 900G**

550g Italian 'oo' pasta flour or plain
  flour
¼ teaspoon sea salt
4 free-range eggs
6 egg yolks
2 tablespoons olive oil

1 To make the pasta, put the flour, salt, eggs, egg yolks and olive oil into a food processor and whiz until the mixture comes together to form coarse crumbs.

2 Tip this into a bowl and gather into a ball with your hands. Turn on to a lightly floured surface and knead well until the pasta dough is smooth and soft, but not sticky. Wrap in cling film and leave to rest for 30 minutes or so.

3 Take a piece of dough about the size of a kiwi fruit; keep the rest well wrapped to stop it drying out. Flatten the piece of dough to a rectangle, about 5mm thick. With the pasta machine set to its thickest setting, feed the dough through two or three times. Adjust the setting by one notch and repeat. Continue in this way, narrowing the setting by one notch each time. The dough will get progressively smoother and more elastic. When you reach the thinnest setting, the pasta is ready to be cut, filled and shaped as required. Repeat with the remaining dough.

4 For ravioli or tortellini, simply cut out the required shapes from the pasta sheets. For tagliatelle, allow the sheets to dry for 10 minutes before cutting – drape them over a clothes airer or the back of a clean chair. Meanwhile fit the pasta machine with the tagliatelle cutters. Pass the dough sheet through the machine cutters, keeping the noodles separate as they emerge. When the pasta sheet has passed through, lift the noodles on to a tray, twirling them into a nest as you do so.

SAFFRON PASTA We use saffron water to give fresh pasta an inviting rich colour and subtle flavour. Our concentrated saffron essence, or saffron water (page 98) as we call it, is the secret here. Simply add a few drops to the mixture as you whiz it in the processor.

cannelloni of tuna with ricotta

Cannelloni are easy to make if you roll the filling in softened pasta sheets rather than stuff dried cannelloni tubes. Here the filling is diced fresh tuna combined with aubergine 'caviar'. I serve the cannelloni topped with a hollandaise lightened with ricotta cheese and gratinéed. **SERVES 4 AS A MAIN COURSE**

1 Preheat the oven to 200°C, Gas 6. Halve the aubergine lengthways, score the flesh and brush with olive oil. Lay the garlic slivers along one cut surface and sandwich together with the other aubergine half. Wrap tightly in foil and bake for 30 minutes or until softened. Cool, then unwrap and scoop out the flesh into a food processor, adding the garlic. Season and whiz to a purée, then tip into a bowl; set aside.

2 Heat 2 tablespoons olive oil in a frying pan, add the shallot and sauté for about 5 minutes to soften. Remove from the heat and cool. Meanwhile, cut the tuna into 1cm dice and place in a bowl. Add the cooled shallot and herbs, then bind with the aubergine purée. Season with salt and pepper to taste.

3 Have ready a large bowl of iced water. Bring a large pan of salted water to the boil and blanch the pasta sheets in two batches, allowing 2 minutes to soften. Remove to the iced water to cool quickly, then drain again. Tear off large sheets of cling film, lay on a board and brush lightly with oil. Lay the drained pasta sheets on top and divide the tuna filling between them, spooning it along one long side. Roll each pasta sheet into a tube, enclosing the filling, then wrap in the cling film, twisting the ends tightly like a cracker so they will be watertight. Chill for about 30 minutes.

4 Meanwhile, make the sauce. Boil the vinegar in a small pan until reduced by half, then immediately pour into a tiny dish. Heat the butter gently until melted, then carefully pour into a jug, leaving the sediment behind. Mix in the olive oil. Put the egg yolks, crushed coriander and 1 tablespoon warm water in a heatproof bowl over a pan of simmering water and beat with a balloon whisk until thickened and creamy. Remove from the heat.

5 Slowly whisk in the butter and oil mixture, drop by drop to begin with, then in a steady trickle, like a mayonnaise. Then beat in the reduced vinegar and lemon juice. Finally beat in the ricotta and lightly whipped cream. Check the seasoning.

6 Bring a large shallow pan of water to the boil, add the cannelloni and boil for 4–5 minutes until they feel firm when pressed. Remove from the water, cool slightly and peel off the cling film.

7 Preheat the grill until very hot. Place the cannelloni, join-side down, in a large ovenproof dish and spoon over the sauce. Sprinkle with the grated Parmesan and grill until golden and bubbling. Serve at once.

8 sheets fresh pasta (page 86)

Filling:
1 small aubergine
2 tablespoons olive oil, plus extra to brush
1 fat garlic clove, thinly sliced
1 large shallot, finely diced
400g fresh tuna
1 tablespoon chopped tarragon
1 tablespoon chopped basil
sea salt and freshly ground pepper

Sauce:
1 tablespoon wine vinegar
50g butter
4 tablespoons olive oil
2 egg yolks
6–8 coriander seeds, crushed
squeeze of lemon juice
100g ricotta cheese
2 tablespoons double cream
1–2 tablespoons freshly grated Parmesan cheese

CHEF'S TIP We cook foods wrapped in cling film to hold them in shape. If you prefer to avoid this technique here, place the cannelloni join-side down in a greased ovenproof dish, cover with foil and bake at 180°C, Gas 4 for 20 minutes. Uncover and proceed as above.

tagliatelle of wild mushrooms

Wild mushrooms have distinctive individual flavours that combine beautifully in sauces. They are largely interchangeable here, so make your selection according to the season. During the summer my favourite Scottish girolles are at their best. Then towards the autumn we get wonderful ceps, trompettes and blewits. I often combine them with Japanese mushrooms, especially shemigi. Or you can use a mixture of wild mushrooms and cultivated chestnut mushrooms for a cheaper option. Fresh wild mushrooms usually contain grit, so they need to be washed carefully. This is a simple pasta dish, which you can embellish with a mushroom velouté for a special occasion. **SERVES 4 AS A MAIN COURSE**

450g fresh tagliatelle, preferably homemade (page 86, ½ quantity)

250–300g selection of wild mushrooms (such as ceps, girolles, blewits, shemigi)

2 tablespoons olive oil

1 shallot, finely chopped

25g butter

100ml double cream

100g wild rocket or baby spinach leaves

sea salt and freshly ground black pepper

To serve:

Mushroom Velouté (see right, optional)

about 50g Parmesan cheese, finely pared into shavings

1 Set the tagliatelle aside while you prepare the mushrooms. Pick over the wild mushrooms and trim the ends. Slice larger ones if necessary. Soak for a few minutes in a bowl of tepid water, swishing with your hands so all debris sinks to the bottom. Lift out the mushrooms and shake well, then pat dry in a large clean tea towel or kitchen paper.

2 Heat the olive oil in a large frying pan, add the shallot and sauté gently for 2 minutes until softened. Add the butter and when it has melted and starts to foam, toss in the cleaned mushrooms. Sauté for about 5 minutes until they are softened. Season to taste, then mix in the cream and cook for a minute or so.

3 Meanwhile, cook the pasta in a large pan of boiling salted water for 1–2 minutes until just *al dente*. Drain and toss with the mushrooms, then add the rocket or spinach and heat until the leaves wilt. Check the seasoning.

4 Divide the mushroom pasta between warmed deep plates or large shallow bowls and pour over the velouté if required. Serve topped with the Parmesan shavings.

CHEF'S SECRET Wild mushroom trimmings are full of flavour, so don't waste them. Spread them on a plate lined with kitchen paper and place in the airing cupboard for a day or until dry and crisp. Or, microwave on a low setting for 5 minutes or so, until crisp. Store in a bag for up to 1 month.

MUSHROOM VELOUTÉ Soak 50g dried mushrooms (morels, ceps, porcini or dried trimmings) in 200ml boiling water for about 10 minutes, then lift out and chop. Strain the liquor through a fine sieve and reserve. Gently sauté 1 finely chopped shallot in 2 tablespoons olive oil until softened but not coloured. Add the mushrooms and 150ml dry white wine. Simmer until reduced by half, then pour in the mushroom liquor and 300ml Brown Chicken Stock (page 210). Bring to the boil and simmer until reduced by half again. Finally, stir in 100ml double cream, return to a simmer and cook for about another 5 minutes. Strain the sauce through a sieve into a jug, pressing with the back of a ladle. Reheat to serve.

CHEF'S SECRET Typically, pasta is tossed with sage leaves that have been fried in butter until frazzled and crisp. My way of serving pasta – in a sage-infused, cream-enriched beurre noisette with shredded fresh sage leaves added at the last moment – gives an altogether different result. None of the fragrance or fresh flavour of the sage is lost.

pumpkin and amaretti ravioli

This ravioli recipe comes from Angela Harnett at The Connaught. It is one that she acquired from her Italian grandmother. Adding a small handful of crushed amaretti to a pumpkin ravioli filling is an Italian custom – it adds a light texture and a hint of sweet almond flavour. I like to serve the ravioli tossed in a sage-infused beurre noisette with shreds of fresh sage, butter and shavings of Parmesan. You will need to cook the pumpkin a day in advance. If possible, track down one of the brown-skinned French variety, which has a full flavour and excellent creamy texture. **SERVES 6–8 AS A MAIN COURSE**

1 Preheat the oven to 180°C, Gas 4. Deseed, peel and chop the pumpkin. Mix with 4 tablespoons olive oil and place on a large sheet of foil. Season and draw the foil up over the pumpkin. Place the foil parcel on a baking tray and bake for up to 1 hour until the flesh is soft. Cool slightly, then whiz in a food processor until smooth. Spoon into a large sieve placed over a bowl. Cool, then refrigerate overnight to allow excess liquid to drain away.

2 The next day, tip the drained pumpkin into a bowl. Finely grate half of the Parmesan. Sauté the shallots in the remaining olive oil for 5 minutes to soften, then mix into the pumpkin flesh together with the breadcrumbs, grated Parmesan and seasoning. Crush three of the biscuits and mix these in too. Set aside.

3 Cut the pasta into 8 pieces and roll into balls; keep wrapped until ready to roll. Using a pasta machine, roll each pasta ball into a long sheet, about 80 x 13cm (see Homemade Pasta, page 86). Repeat with the rest and keep covered with a clean tea towel.

4 Shape the ravioli (see overleaf) and place on a tray lined with a clean tea towel. Chill in the refrigerator, uncovered, until ready to serve. Pare the remaining piece of Parmesan into fine shavings. Crush the last of the amaretti and set aside.

5 To make the sage beurre noisette, strip the leaves from the sage stalks and set aside. Put the unsalted butter in a saucepan with the sage stalks and melt slowly, then increase the heat and cook until the moment the butter starts to turn brown. Immediately take off the heat and leave to stand for 1 minute. Slowly strain the butter through a fine sieve into a clean pan, leaving the sediment behind. Discard the sage stalks. Shred the sage leaves as finely as you can. Return the beurre noisette to a low heat and stir in the cream, then take off the heat and add the shredded sage leaves.

6 Meanwhile, bring a large pan of lightly salted water to the boil, add the ravioli and cook for 2 minutes. Drain and return to the pan. Add the sage beurre noisette and seasoning, and toss gently to mix.

7 Serve in warmed shallow bowls, scattered with the last of the crushed amaretti and Parmesan shavings.

1 quantity homemade saffron pasta dough (page 86)
1 egg yolk, beaten with 1 teaspoon cold water

Filling and to serve:
1.5kg wedge fresh pumpkin
6 tablespoons olive oil
150g Parmesan cheese
2 large shallots, chopped
100g fresh white breadcrumbs
4 amaretti biscuits
sea salt and freshly ground black pepper

Sage beurre noisette:
6 sage sprigs, plus stalks
75g unsalted butter, in pieces
2 tablespoons double cream

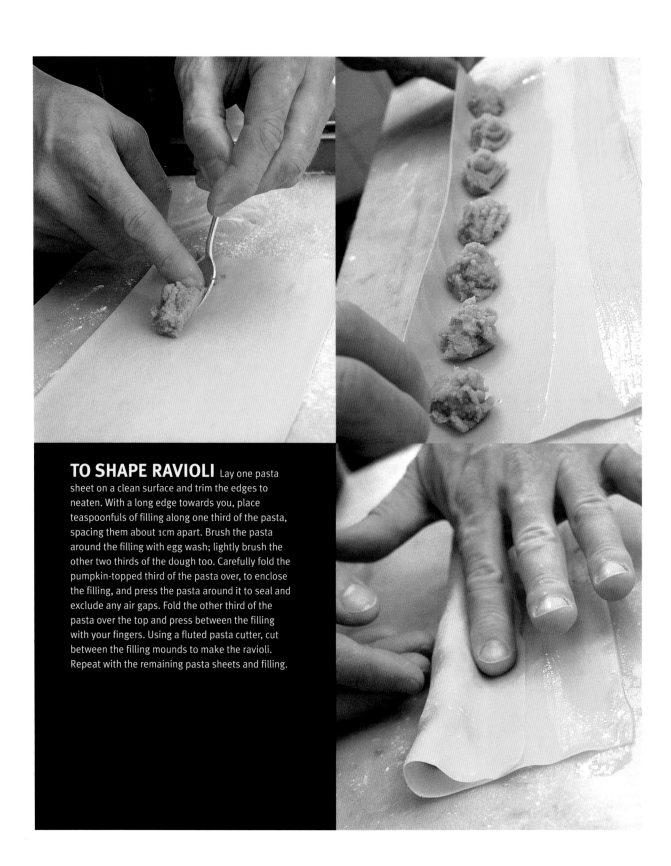

TO SHAPE RAVIOLI Lay one pasta sheet on a clean surface and trim the edges to neaten. With a long edge towards you, place teaspoonfuls of filling along one third of the pasta, spacing them about 1cm apart. Brush the pasta around the filling with egg wash; lightly brush the other two thirds of the dough too. Carefully fold the pumpkin-topped third of the pasta over, to enclose the filling, and press the pasta around it to seal and exclude any air gaps. Fold the other third of the pasta over the top and press between the filling with your fingers. Using a fluted pasta cutter, cut between the filling mounds to make the ravioli. Repeat with the remaining pasta sheets and filling.

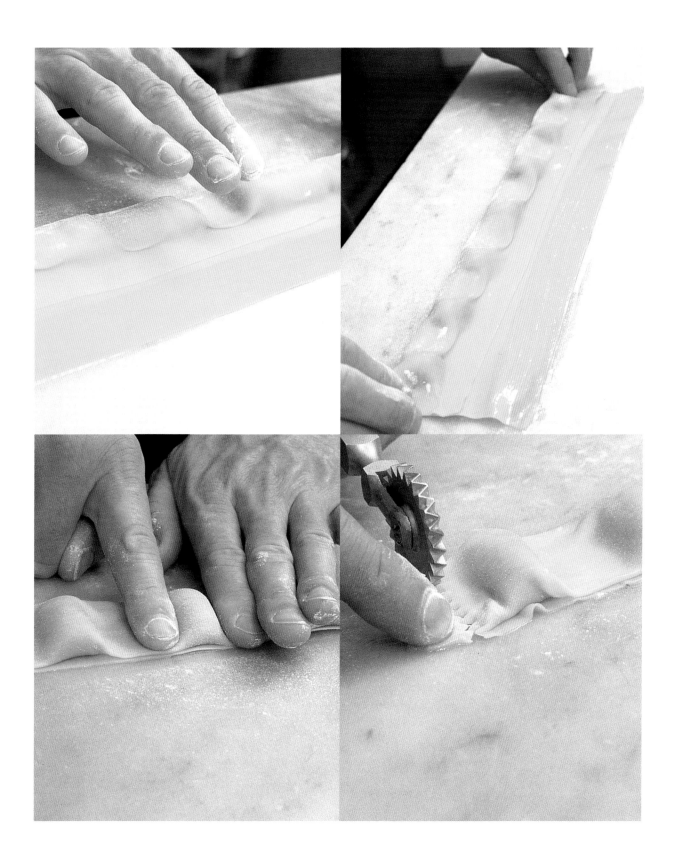

smoked haddock and asparagus open ravioli

Fresh pasta rounds are layered with a light, creamy sauce of smoked haddock and asparagus tips, then served topped with lightly poached quail's eggs, for a new take on lasagne. Serve simply as an elegant lunch, or make a delicate asparagus velouté with the trimmings and spoon around the pasta ensemble for a special occasion. **SERVES 4 AS A STARTER OR LIGHT MEAL**

1 Using a 7–8cm plain cutter, cut out 12 rounds from the pasta sheets, then cover and set aside until ready to cook.
2 Poach the smoked haddock fillet in the milk for about 5–7 minutes until the flesh is just beginning to flake. Remove the fish from the milk and leave until cool enough to handle, then skin and flake the flesh.
3 Cut the stalks from the asparagus spears, leaving about 10cm tips. Reserve the asparagus stalks for the velouté. Blanch the tips in salted water for 1–2 minutes until just tender, then drain and plunge into a bowl of ice cold water to refresh.
4 Put the crème fraîche into a small pan, heat gently, then add the flaked haddock, asparagus tips and chives, and heat through. Check the seasoning.
5 Meanwhile, cook the pasta in a pan of boiling water for 1–2 minutes until *al dente*, then drain and toss with the melted butter. At the same time, if using quail's eggs, cook in a small pan of boiling water for 1–1½ minutes until lightly cooked. Drain and shell, then carefully coat with a little of the creamy sauce base.
6 To assemble, place a round of pasta on each warmed plate. Add a layer of the asparagus and haddock sauce, then another pasta round. Repeat these layers, then top with the quail's eggs and spoon over a little more sauce. Serve immediately, with asparagus velouté if you like.

about 225g fresh pasta sheets, preferably homemade (page 86, ¼ quantity)

Filling:
1 large Finnan or undyed smoked haddock fillet, about 400g
500ml milk
300g thin asparagus spears
200g crème fraîche
1 tablespoon chopped chives
25g butter, melted
12 quail's eggs (optional)
sea salt and freshly ground black pepper

To serve:
Asparagus Velouté (see right, optional)

ASPARAGUS VELOUTÉ Chop the reserved asparagus stalks finely and sauté with 1 finely chopped large shallot in 2 tablespoons olive oil for about 5 minutes until softened. Add a handful baby spinach leaves and the chopped leaves from a sprig of tarragon. Cook until wilted, then pour in 300ml Fish Stock (page 209). Bring to the boil, lower the heat and simmer for 10 minutes. Whiz in a blender or food processor, then pass through a sieve, rubbing with the back of a ladle. Return the sauce to the pan and stir in 2 tablespoons double cream. Reheat gently to serve.

spatzle

This is the German answer to pasta, but it's easier to prepare. You simply make a thick eggy batter, rub it through a slotted plate or colander directly into a pan of boiling water and the batter sets instantly into soft doughy squiggles. Once they are cooked and drained, I fry the spatzle in beurre noisette so they puff up, become crispy and turn golden brown. Serve as an accompaniment to rich meat and game stews, or with a light tomato sauce and freshly grated Parmesan for a light meal.

SERVES 4–6 AS AN ACCOMPANIMENT OR LIGHT MEAL

1 Sift the flour and salt together into a large bowl. Gradually beat in the eggs, then the water, until you have a batter with a thick pouring consistency. If necessary, add a little extra water. Allow to rest for 2 hours. In the meantime, make the beurre noisette (see below).

2 When ready to cook, bring a large pan of water to the boil. Have ready a large bowl of iced water. Place a spatzle plate or colander over the pan of boiling water.

3 You will need to cook the spatzle in batches. Ladle some runny dough on to the plate and immediately rub through, using a dough scraper or the back of the ladle. As soon as the dough is through, remove the plate. When they are just cooked, the spatzle will rise to the surface. Allow them a few more seconds, then lift out with a slotted spoon into the bowl of iced water. Repeat in batches until the dough is used up. Drain and dry on kitchen paper.

4 Fry the spatzle in batches. Heat a quarter of the beurre noisette in a large frying pan, add half the spatzle and fry until lightly browned. Add another quarter of the butter and continue to fry until the spatzle are puffed up and crispy. Season generously with salt, pepper and nutmeg to taste. Drain on kitchen paper and keep warm while you fry the rest. Serve hot, sprinkled with chopped herbs.

250g plain flour or 'oo' pasta flour
1 teaspoon fine sea salt
4 medium eggs, beaten
about 3 tablespoons cold water
100g Beurre Noisette (see below)
freshly grated nutmeg, to taste
sea salt and freshly ground black pepper
finely chopped herbs (parsley, basil or chervil), to serve

BEURRE NOISETTE Heat 125g unsalted butter slowly in a saucepan, then increase the heat and cook until the moment it starts to turn brown. Immediately take off the heat and leave to stand for 1 minute. Then slowly pour the golden brown butter into a heatproof bowl, leaving the sediment behind.

my saffron shellfish risotto

Preparing a classic, creamy risotto by the traditional method can take up to 20 minutes with constant attention, and this isn't a dish you can prepare ahead and reheat successfully. We don't test our clients' patience in the restaurant, neither need you keep your guests waiting at home if you adopt my risotto technique (described below and illustrated overleaf). It halves the cooking time. Of the different varieties of risotto rice available, my personal favourite is Carnaroli because the grains are plump and remain firm. **SERVES 4 AS A STARTER OR LIGHT MEAL**

200g risotto rice (Carnaroli, Arborio or Vialone Nano)

20 langoustine tails, or 200g raw tiger prawns (heads removed)

100g podded fresh baby broad beans

about 500ml Chicken Stock (page 210) or Fish Stock (page 209)

3 tablespoons olive oil

1 large or 3 smaller shallots, finely chopped

4 tablespoons dry white wine

50g butter, chilled and cubed

1 teaspoon saffron water (see below)

1 tablespoon finely chopped chervil

1 tablespoon finely chopped chives

2 tablespoons freshly grated Parmesan cheese

sea salt and freshly ground black pepper

Parmesan cheese shavings, to serve

1 Bring a large pan of salted water to the boil. Add the rice and blanch the grains for 5 minutes, then drain and spread out on a tray. Cover and set aside until ready to cook, or chill if you are several hours ahead of serving.

2 Prepare the langoustines (see page 20), or if using prawns, peel and remove the dark intestinal thread. Set the peeled langoustine tails or prawns aside.

3 Blanch the baby broad beans in boiling water for 2–3 minutes, then drain and slip the beans out of their skins. Season and set aside.

4 Bring the stock to a simmer in a pan. Meanwhile, heat the olive oil in a larger pan and sauté the shallot for 3 minutes until softened, then stir in the rice. Cook for about 2 minutes, stirring frequently. Add the wine and reduce right down.

5 Now add one third of the stock and stir frequently until the stock is almost all absorbed. Add another third of the stock, and stir until absorbed. Add half of the remaining stock, then add the broad beans and stir gently. Once this stock is absorbed, check the rice grains. If they are still a little chalky, then add more stock. (This stage only takes around 10 minutes.)

6 In the meantime, heat half the butter in a frying pan until it starts to foam. Add the langoustine tails or prawns and stir-fry until bright pink and firm, about 3 minutes. Season and set aside.

7 When the risotto is creamy and the rice is *al dente* (cooked, but retaining a bite), stir in the saffron water, followed by the herbs and Parmesan. Finally, stir in the remaining butter and check the seasoning.

8 Divide the risotto between warmed bowls. Arrange the langoustines or tiger prawns on top and scatter with Parmesan shavings. Serve immediately.

SAFFRON WATER We buy Spanish saffron and make a concentrated essence by crushing saffron strands into a little boiling water. The infused 'saffron water' gives risottos and pasta dishes an exotic flavour and rich colour. To make this, mix 1 teaspoon of saffron strands with 3–4 tablespoons boiling water, then cool. Keep in a jar in the fridge for up to 3 days, or freeze as tiny ice cubes, and use as required.

THE PERFECT RISOTTO Heat the
oil in a medium heavy-based pan and sauté the
shallot for 3 minutes until softened, then stir in the
rice and cook for about 2 minutes, stirring
frequently. Add the wine and reduce right down.
Now add one third of the stock and stir frequently
until the stock is almost all absorbed. Add another
third of the stock, and stir until absorbed.
Add half of the remaining stock, then add the broad
beans and stir gently. Once this stock is absorbed,
check the rice grains. If they are still a little chalky,
then add more stock. (This stage only takes around
10 minutes.)
When the risotto is creamy and the rice is *al dente*
(cooked, but retaining a bite), stir in the saffron
water, followed by the herbs and Parmesan.
Finally, stir in the remaining butter in cubes.

green herb risotto with sautéed scallops

Scallops have a delicious sweet, creamy flavour that suits different flavourings, from Oriental and spicy to rich red wines. Sautéed scallops are delicious served simply with a green salad, but I also like to serve them with a freshly cooked herb risotto. Full-bodied Barolo, one of the great wines of Italy, is reduced down with port to make a rich glaze for the scallops.

SERVES 4 AS A STARTER OR 2 AS A MAIN DISH

250ml Barolo wine

250ml ruby port

600ml Chicken Stock (page 210) or
   Fish Stock (page 209)

about 4 tablespoons olive oil

1 shallot, finely chopped

200g risotto rice (Carnaroli, Arborio
   or Vialone Nano)

4 tablespoons dry white wine

6 king scallops, cleaned (see page 19)

large knob of butter

1 tablespoon chopped tarragon

1 tablespoon chopped basil

1 tablespoon chopped chives

sea salt and freshly ground black
   pepper

extra chopped herbs, to serve

1 First, make your reduction. Pour the Barolo and port into a saucepan and bring to the boil. Bubble until reduced to about 4 tablespoons, to make a syrupy glaze. Set aside to cool.

2 To make the risotto, bring the stock to a simmer in a saucepan. Meanwhile, heat 2 tablespoons olive oil in a deep saucepan and sauté the shallot for about 5 minutes until softened. Add the rice and cook for 2 minutes until the grains are opaque. Pour in the white wine and cook until reduced right down.

3 Add a quarter of the simmering stock and cook, stirring until it is all absorbed. Add the remaining stock, a ladleful at a time, making sure each addition is absorbed before adding another. This should take about 15 minutes, by which time the rice will be tender but still have a good bite. You may not need to add all of the stock. Season with salt and pepper to taste.

4 When the risotto is almost cooked, heat a heavy-based frying pan or ridged griddle until you feel a good heat rising. Add a thin film of olive oil, then place the scallops in the pan, in a circle. Cook for 1½ minutes, then turn (in the same order you placed them in the pan to ensure even cooking). Cook the other side for a minute or so, until golden. Press the scallops with the back of a fork: if they feel slightly springy they are ready. Remove to a warmed plate and allow to rest while you finish the risotto.

5 Stir the butter and chopped herbs into the risotto. Warm the red wine and port glaze. Slice each scallop in half horizontally. Spoon the risotto into shallow bowls, arrange the scallops on top and trickle over the glaze. Drizzle with a little olive oil and scatter with extra chopped herbs. Serve immediately.

whole spice basmati pilaff

This is an easy pilaff, which is simply left to cook in the oven. The whole spices can be removed before serving if you like, leaving the rice white and glistening but also fragrant and delicious. Alternatively, you can omit the spices and flavour the pilaff simply with herbs and lemon zest. Use best quality basmati rice. A round cast-iron casserole is the ideal cooking pot; a roasting tin is not suitable. **SERVES 4–6 AS AN ACCOMPANIMENT**

1 Rinse the rice (see below). Preheat the oven to 180°C, Gas 4. Make a cartouche to fit a medium round casserole dish: cut a circle of greaseproof slightly larger than the dish and snip a tiny hole in the centre to make a steam vent.

2 Melt two thirds of the butter in the flameproof casserole dish and sauté the onion for about 5 minutes until softened. Add the rice and stir well, then add the herbs, whole spices and lemon or orange zest. Cook for a minute or two.

3 Bring the stock to the boil, using the larger volume if you prefer a more tender grain. Mix the stock into the rice along with the salt and pepper to taste. Press on the cartouche, turning the edges up and pressing them to the side of the pan for a neat fit. Make sure the vent is visible. There is no need to cover with a lid.

4 Bake in the oven for about 25 minutes. Remove from the oven, allow to stand for 5 minutes, and then remove the cartouche. Fork through the remaining butter until the rice grains are fluffy and separate, removing the whole spices before serving if you prefer.

250g basmati rice

75g butter

1 large onion, finely chopped

1 large thyme sprig

1 bay leaf

2 cinnamon sticks

6 cardamom pods, split open

2 star anise (optional)

2 cloves

finely pared zest of 1 lemon or
   orange, in pieces

500–600ml Chicken Stock (page 210)
   or water

1 teaspoon sea salt

freshly ground black pepper

BASMATI RICE This fragrant rice is best washed to remove excess starch and lighten the grain. Put the rice into a large bowl, half-fill with cold running water and swish the rice grains with your fingers. Tip out the water leaving the wet grains behind. Repeat twice more until the water runs clear, then drain the rice in a sieve. Set aside.

Vegetables

The passport of my menus is the seasonality of vegetables, not fish or meat. Of course, it's now possible to ignore the seasons and buy in the same vegetables all year round, but the ethics, flavour and diversity of seasonal vegetables makes for a far more interesting menu.

I focus hard on homegrown produce, perhaps fuelled by my childhood experiences. School holidays were often spent picking vegetables for money. Our home in Shipston-on-Stour was close to the market gardens in the Vale of Evesham. I associate early spring with cutting green asparagus stems, not for our own use but for the growers to bunch and sell on. We lunched on fresh asparagus soup made, no doubt, from trimmings, so I grew up with a taste for it.

As a teenager I was passionate about fishing, but times were not easy for us as a family then. Bank holiday weekends coincided with the potato harvest, so we would go camping to Broadstairs in Kent and pick potatoes for money. I found that if I fixed sacks between my legs and shovelled in spuds as fast as I could on the Saturday, I could earn enough in a day to spend Sunday fishing off Margate Pier.

As a consequence of my youth, I have learnt to hate waste. How stupid to turn potatoes into silly barrel shapes and waste good flesh. Why throw asparagus trimmings away when they can be turned into amazing soup? I love to feel fresh spears between my fingers as I consider how to cook them. The short intimate season of white asparagus is, to my mind, on a par with the fleeting appearance of white truffle.

watercress and potato soup

This is one of those invaluable recipes that can be built on and taken to new heights each time you make it. At its simplest, it is a fresh tasting, velvety smooth soup, that's delicious served hot, topped with a dollop of crème fraîche. Or, you can serve it chilled as a refreshing summer soup, infused with olive oil ice cubes if you like – to keep it cool and impart flavour as they slowly melt. For a special occasion, float a poached egg in the centre of each serving and top with a spoonful of caviar (as illustrated) – you break the softly set egg into the soup as you eat it. Or if you prefer, simply garnish each portion with a poached oyster. **SERVES 2 AS A STARTER**

1 litre Vegetable Nage (page 211)

1 teaspoon vegetable bouillon
   powder

2 tablespoons olive oil

1 large shallot, finely chopped

200g waxy potatoes (such as
   Charlotte), peeled and finely
   chopped

250g watercress, well washed

small handful of baby spinach leaves

sea salt and freshly ground back
   pepper

To serve:

either 2 tablespoons crème fraîche,
   lightly whipped

or 4 medium poached eggs (see
   page 140) and 25g can caviar

or 4 poached oysters

plus olive oil, to drizzle

1 For the stock, bring the vegetable nage to the boil, sprinkle in the bouillon powder and stir until dissolved.

2 Heat the olive oil in a large saucepan and gently sauté the shallot and potatoes for 5–7 minutes until softened. Do not allow them to colour.

3 Pour in the vegetable stock and bring to a rolling boil, then drop in the watercress and spinach. As soon as the leaves wilt, remove the pan from the heat and transfer the leaves and potato to a food processor, using a slotted spoon; reserve the liquor.

4 Whiz the mixture until smooth, adding the liquor back gradually. This is best done in stages to ensure a very smooth texture. Chill until required (unless you are serving the soup hot and straightaway).

5 To serve hot, reheat the soup (if necessary). For a simple finish, ladle into warmed bowls and top with a dollop of crème fraîche. For a more elaborate finish, slide a poached egg into each portion and top with a spoonful of caviar. Alternatively, float a poached oyster on each serving.

6 To serve chilled, divide the soup between chilled bowls, drizzle with a little olive oil and add a few olive oil ice cubes to each serving if you like.

INFUSED ICE CUBES Use 500ml Vegetable Nage (page 211). Pour three quarters into ice cube trays, to fill about 20 cavities. Freeze until solid around the edges, but still partially liquid in the centre. Using the tip of a small teaspoon, hollow out the centre of each cube and pour in about 1 teaspoon olive oil. Carefully pour in a little more stock to cover and freeze until solid. The oil should be trapped inside each ice cube, like a bubble. Use straight from the freezer.

CHEF'S SECRET If I am serving this soup warm topped with poached eggs, I find it less of a hassle to prepare them in advance. Follow the instructions for poaching eggs on page 140. When ready to serve, simply place a poached egg in each portion – the heat of the soup will be sufficient to warm the eggs through.

asparagus soup with truffle cream

Make this soup in the spring when homegrown asparagus is in season and available at a good price. You don't need to seek out young, tender spears – it's the flavour you need, not the texture. You will achieve a good result with a combination of stalks and trimmings, so don't discard the woody ends and peelings if you're preparing asparagus to serve as a vegetable – use them here. Adding a couple of handfuls of tender spinach leaves helps to boost the natural asparagus colour without detracting from the flavour. **SERVES 4 AS A STARTER**

1kg green asparagus (including
   trimmings if available)
75g butter
1 onion, chopped
1 fat garlic clove, chopped
750ml Chicken Stock (page 210) or
   Vegetable Nage (page 211)
100g baby leaf spinach
sea salt and freshly ground black
   pepper

To serve:
150ml double cream
½ teaspoon truffle oil
2 teaspoons finely chopped chives

1 Chop the asparagus into small even-sized pieces. Heat the butter in a large saucepan and, when it starts to sizzle, add the onion and garlic. Sauté gently for about 10 minutes until softened but not coloured. Add the asparagus pieces and sauté for a further 5–10 minutes until softened.

2 Meanwhile, bring the chicken stock or vegetable nage to the boil in another pan.

3 Pour the hot stock over the asparagus, season to taste and simmer for 3 minutes. Then stir in the spinach and cook briefly, until just wilted. Immediately remove from the heat and strain the stock, reserving the vegetables.

4 Purée the vegetables in a blender or food processor, gradually adding the stock back until you have a creamy liquid. Pass the soup through a sieve into a clean pan (or bowl if you are not serving straightaway, see below). Rub the pulp in the sieve with the back of a ladle to extract as much flavour as possible.

5 To serve, lightly whip the cream with the truffle oil and seasoning until softly peaking. Reheat the soup gently until almost at a simmer, but do not boil or you will destroy the amazing colour and flavour. Serve in warmed bowls topped with dollops of truffle cream and chopped chives.

CHEF'S SECRET In the restaurant we prepare this soup ahead, as you probably will if you're entertaining. The trick is to capture the freshness and colour of the asparagus. To achieve this, we cool the puréed soup as quickly as possible, by pouring it straight from the blender into a bowl that is held in a larger bowl containing plenty of ice cubes and a little water. When the soup is cold, remove from the bowl of ice, cover and chill until required.

my roasted tomato soup

A superlative fresh tomato soup is one of the hallmarks of a good cook. My secret is to first roast the tomatoes, together with onions and herbs. Flavourful tomatoes are, of course, essential. To enhance the flavour I add smoked sun-dried cherry tomatoes with a hickory flavour. If you can't find these, substitute snipped soft sun-dried tomatoes and a dash of barbecue sauce. (Illustrated overleaf)

SERVES 4 AS A STARTER

1 Preheat the oven to 220°C, Gas 7. Pour the olive oil into a roasting tin and heat in the oven until almost smoking. Carefully tip in the tomatoes, onion rings and garlic, then toss to coat in the oil. Scatter over the thyme sprigs, sprinkle with sugar and season generously with salt and pepper. Roast in the oven for 20–25 minutes until nicely caramelised, stirring once or twice and adding the basil towards the end of cooking.

2 Tip the roasted tomatoes and flavourings into a saucepan, discarding any woody thyme stalks. Bring the stock to the boil in another pan, then pour over the tomatoes. Bring to the boil, add the smoked tomatoes (or semi-soft sun-dried tomatoes plus barbecue sauce) and cook for 5 minutes.

3 Strain the stock, reserving the tomato mixture. Tip the tomatoes into a blender or food processor and whiz, gradually adding the stock back in, until smooth and creamy. Pass the soup through a sieve into a clean pan or bowl, rubbing with the back of a ladle. Taste and adjust the seasoning.

4 For the garnish, heat the olive oil in a frying pan. Snip the vine tomatoes into four clusters and fry them on the vine for about a minute.

5 Reheat the soup if necessary, but it's best served warm rather than piping hot. Pour into warmed bowls and top with the pan-roasted vine tomatoes. Drizzle the pan juices around the tomatoes and scatter with basil leaves.

4 tablespoons olive oil

1kg plum tomatoes, halved

1 onion, thinly sliced

2 fat garlic cloves, halved

small handful of thyme sprigs

1 teaspoon caster sugar

small handful of basil sprigs

1 litre Chicken Stock (page 210) or
   Vegetable Nage (page 211)

3 smoked sun-dried cherry tomatoes
   in oil, drained (or 2 semi-soft sun-
   dried tomatoes and 1 tablespoon
   barbecue sauce)

sea salt and freshly ground black
   pepper

To serve:

2 tablespoons olive oil

200–300g baby cherry tomatoes on
   the vine

small basil leaves

CHEF'S TIP For a really velvety texture, use a blender rather than a food processor to purée a creamed soup. To ensure a perfectly smooth result, pass the puréed soup through a sieve.

Vegetables   111

pan-roasted pumpkin salad with ricotta and croûtons

Pumpkins are in season during the autumn and, of course, they are everywhere around Hallowe'en. Pumpkin flesh has a delectable sweet, creamy flavour that lends itself beautifully to tasty soups, fillings for ravioli (see page 91), and pureés to accompany rich meats and game. Chopped and pan-roasted, it forms the basis of a fabulous starter salad. I prefer the brown-skinned ridged pumpkins – popular in France and the West Indies. These are often sold here in thick wedges, but you can use a small round 'jack-o-lantern' pumpkin if you like. Pumpkin oil is available from healthfood shops. Dark golden in colour with a warm nutty aroma, it makes a tasty addition to salad dressings and is ideal for trickling over warm vegetables.

SERVES 4 AS A STARTER

1 small, ripe pumpkin, or about 1kg unpeeled weight

about 150g mixed sharp salad leaves, such as frisée and wild rocket

4–5 tablespoons olive oil, plus extra to brush

50g butter

½ small ciabatta or baguette

4 tablespoons Vinaigrette (page 218)

4 tablespoons pumpkin seeds, toasted

3–5 tablespoons ricotta cheese

2 tablespoons balsamic vinegar

1 tablespoon pumpkin oil

sea salt and freshly ground black pepper

about 25g Parmesan cheese, finely pared into shavings, to serve

1 Peel the pumpkin: the easiest way to do this is to cut it into wedges first, with a heavy-bladed knife. Then scoop out the seeds and stringy membrane and peel off the skin, using a short, sharp knife. Chop the flesh into 1cm cubes and season with salt and pepper.

2 Separate the frisée leaves, then tear into smaller pieces. Wash the frisée and rocket, dry well and place in a large bowl.

3 Heat the olive oil in a large frying pan, add the pumpkin cubes and sauté for about 5 minutes. Add the butter and cook, shaking the pan constantly, for a further 3–4 minutes until the pumpkin cubes are nicely caramelised and softened. Remove and drain on kitchen paper; allow to cool slightly.

4 Meanwhile, slice the ciabatta or baguette thinly and brush with olive oil. Lightly toast on both sides until crisp.

5 Lightly dress the salad leaves with the vinaigrette. Add the warm pumpkin cubes and pumpkin seeds, and toss gently to mix, seasoning to taste. Divide between serving plates. Spread the ciabatta toasts with the ricotta, season and place alongside the salad. Drizzle the balsamic vinegar and pumpkin oil over, and scatter with Parmesan shavings to serve.

CHEF'S TIP For optimum flavour it's important to use a really ripe pumpkin here – bright golden flesh indicates that the vegetable is ripe and ready to cook. Roasting in the pan or oven gives a firmer texture and more pronounced flavour than boiling pumpkin.

herb gnocchi with tomato salsa

This recipe is all about getting extra flavour into a simple dish. Rather than boil and mash potatoes in the usual way for gnocchi, I bake them for a fuller flavour and fluffier texture, then mash. Sautéeing the gnocchi in oil and butter before serving crisps the surface and gives them a delicious flavour. **SERVES 2 AS A MAIN COURSE, 4 AS A LIGHT MEAL OR STARTER**

2 large baking potatoes, about
　400g each

160g plain flour

1 teaspoon fine sea salt

1 tablespoon chopped basil

1 tablespoon chopped parsley

1 large free-range egg, beaten

4 tablespoons olive oil, plus extra to
　drizzle

50g butter

Tomato salsa:

6 vine-ripened plum tomatoes

1 small red onion, finely chopped

2 spring onions, finely sliced

juice of 1 lime

1 tablespoon sesame oil

generous dash of Tabasco

1 tablespoon finely chopped basil

1 tablespoon finely chopped
　coriander

sea salt and freshly ground black
　pepper

CHEF'S SECRET Cutting the dough with the thicker edge of a knife has the effect of blunting the ends and gives the gnocchi their characteristic pinched edges. Cook the gnocchi as soon as you have cut them, so they don't dry out.

1 Preheat the oven to 180°C, Gas 4. Scrub the potatoes, but don't score or slit them. Bake for about 1¼ hours until soft in the centre when pierced with a skewer. Set aside to cool for 10 minutes, then peel off the skins. Mash the potato flesh in a bowl or press through a potato ricer, then leave to cool completely.

2 When the mash is cool, mix in the flour and salt until evenly incorporated, then add the herbs. Gradually work in the beaten egg until you have a smooth, firm dough – you may not need to add all of it.

3 Bring a large pan of salted water to the boil. Have ready a large bowl of iced water. Divide the dough into 8 balls, then roll each out on a lightly floured surface to a long, narrow sausage, about 30cm long, and flatten very slightly to make an oval shape. Cut the rolls, slightly on the diagonal, into 3cm lengths, using the back of a table knife or thick cook's knife.

4 Cook the gnocchi in batches. Add about a quarter of them to the boiling water and cook for 2–3 minutes, until they rise to the surface. Lift out with a slotted spoon and place in the bowl of iced water. Leave for a minute or so, then drain well and pat dry with kitchen paper. Repeat to cook the remaining gnocchi, always returning the water to a rolling boil in between.

5 When all the gnocchi are cooked and cooled, combine them in a bowl. Drizzle with a little olive oil to keep them separate, then cover with cling film and chill until required.

6 To make the salsa, dip the tomatoes in boiling water for 30 seconds or so to loosen the skins, then into cold water to refresh; drain and peel away the skins. Quarter, core and deseed the tomatoes. Finely chop the flesh and place in a bowl with the other salsa ingredients. Toss to mix and season well, then spoon into a serving dish.

7 When ready to serve, heat 2 tablespoons olive oil and half the butter in a large frying pan until hot. Sauté the gnocchi, in batches, for 3–4 minutes until golden brown and crispy on both sides. Drain on kitchen paper and keep warm, uncovered in a low oven, while you sauté the rest of the gnocchi, using the remaining oil and butter as needed. Serve with the tomato salsa.

torte of field mushrooms

These impressive tortes are a vegetarian version of a popular starter on the menu at Claridges. You will need to buy 12 large grilling mushrooms – portobello mushrooms are ideal and widely available. Served with a leafy salad, this is an ideal main course if you are entertaining vegetarians. **SERVES 4 AS A MAIN COURSE**

1 First, make the pancake batter. Whiz the flour, salt, egg and milk in a blender or food processor until smooth. Pour into a jug and leave to rest in the fridge.

2 Preheat the oven to 190ºC, Gas 5. To prepare the large mushrooms, wipe clean with a damp cloth, but don't wash or peel them. Cut off the stalks (save for the duxelle if you like). Brush the tops with the melted butter and place, cap-side up, in a roasting tin. Season with salt and pepper and bake for 10 minutes. Leave to cool in the tin, then drain off any juices and chill.

3 Meanwhile, prepare the mushroom duxelle. Chop the mushrooms as finely as possible – by hand or by pulsing in a food processor. Heat the butter and oil in a frying pan until really hot, then add the mushrooms and stir-fry over a high heat until softened and cooked. Season to taste, and add the tarragon and sherry or Madeira. The duxelle should be soft, but quite dry (if necessary cook for a little longer to evaporate any liquid). Cool, then mix in the breadcrumbs and egg yolk.

4 Stir the melted butter into the pancake batter. Heat a 15cm crêpe pan and oil lightly. Cook the pancakes, making them as thin and lacy as possible – you should make 10–12. Set aside the 4 thinnest pancakes to cool (freeze the rest).

5 Now, layer the whole baked mushrooms and duxelle. Trim the baked mushrooms to the same size, using a 7cm cutter if necessary. Spoon half the duxelle evenly on top of 4 mushrooms. Cover each with another mushroom, then another layer of duxelle, and finally top with the remaining mushrooms.

6 Wrap each mushroom sandwich in a pancake (they won't be completely enclosed). Place join-side down on a plate and refrigerate.

7 Set the oven to 200ºC, Gas 6. Roll out the pastry (half at a time for easy handling) on a lightly floured board to a 3mm thickness. Cut out four 12cm rounds and four 15cm rounds. Brush round the edges with egg wash. Put the mushroom pancake parcels on the smaller rounds and cover with the larger ones. Cup one parcel upside-down in your hand and carefully press the edges together, then trim to leave a 1cm edge. Crimp this with a fork. Repeat to shape the rest of the tortes.

8 Place the tortes flat-side down on a non-stick baking sheet. Score the pastry with the tip of a thin knife, radiating from the centre but don't cut right through. Brush all over with egg wash and rest in the fridge for 15 minutes or so.

9 Bake the tortes for 20 minutes or until puffed and golden brown. Leave on the baking sheet for 10 minutes, then carefully slide on to plates. Serve with a salad.

12 large flat mushrooms, at least 8cm
   diameter
60g butter, melted
olive oil, for frying
500g Puff Pastry (page 190), or
   ready-made puff
1 egg yolk, beaten with 1 teaspoon
   cold water (egg wash), to glaze
sea salt and freshly ground black
   pepper

Pancake batter:
100g plain flour
pinch of salt
1 free-range medium egg
250ml milk
1 tablespoon melted butter

Mushroom duxelle:
150g chestnut mushrooms, or wild
   mushrooms as available
50g butter
1 tablespoon olive oil
1 teaspoon chopped tarragon
1 tablespoon sherry or Madeira
30g fresh white breadcrumbs
1 egg yolk

assiette de legumes with thyme velouté

Vegetarian dishes are an increasingly popular choice in my restaurants and I enjoy creating new medleys of vegetables that enhance their fabulous colours and flavours. This simple, but sophisticated selection of vegetables is served with a light thyme velouté. Vary the vegetables according to the season and personal preference – you might like to serve more of a smaller selection of varieties. Prepare each vegetable separately as described, ready to reheat and serve. You will need a large pan of lightly salted water for blanching and a big bowl of iced water for refreshing. Make sure there's plenty of ice in the freezer to keep the refreshing water cool. **SERVES 2 AS A MAIN COURSE, 4 AS A LIGHT MEAL OR STARTER**

Confit of tomatoes Set the oven to the lowest setting (80–100°C). Dip the tomatoes into boiling water for 30 seconds or so, then into iced water. Drain and slip off the skins, then quarter and deseed. Lay cut-side down in a shallow roasting tin and cover with olive oil. Add slivers of garlic, thyme and basil sprigs. Place in the oven for about 1½ hours until the flesh is soft but intact. Season and cool in the oil, then drain well.

Asparagus Trim the base of the stalks and peel the lower third with a swivel vegetable peeler. Blanch the spears in boiling water for 2 minutes, then remove to a bowl of iced water.

Braised lettuces Halve lengthways and sauté, cut-side down, in a little olive oil for 1–2 minutes. Season lightly and pour in vegetable nage to a depth of 1cm. Cover with a butter paper and cook over a medium heat for 5 minutes until just tender (the nage will have reduced down to a glaze). Cool.

Peas and broad beans Pod these and slip the broad beans out of their skins. Blanch for 2 minutes and refresh in iced water.

Baby artichokes Trim the stalks and halve the artichoke hearts lengthways. Drop into cold water acidulated with the vitamin C powder or lemon juice. Drain and pat dry when ready to cook. Heat a little olive oil in a small frying pan and sauté the artichokes for 2–3 minutes. Pour in 300ml vegetable nage and simmer for 15–20 minutes until tender. Remove, cool slightly, then scrape out the small hairy choke on the base. Cool and pat dry.

Baby turnips Blanch for 3 minutes or until just tender, then refresh.

Sautéed wild mushrooms Trim the stalk bases, rinse the mushrooms quickly in cold water, drain and pat dry. Heat a thin layer of olive oil in a pan and sauté the mushrooms over a high heat until just tender. Season lightly and set aside.

TO SERVE Reheat the asparagus, turnips, lettuce, peas and broad beans quickly and separately in a little hot nage with a little butter for up to 1 minute. Sauté the artichokes and mushrooms separately and briefly in a little olive oil until hot. The tomatoes can be served at room temperature. Reheat the velouté and pour into a jug. Arrange the vegetables on serving plates and accompany with the velouté.

2–3 plum tomatoes

2 fat garlic cloves, thinly sliced

2 thyme sprigs

2 basil sprigs

200g green or white asparagus spears, or a mixture of both

2 Little Gem lettuces

100g peas or baby broad beans, or a mixture of both

4 baby artichoke hearts

6–8 baby turnips, quartered unless tiny

200g mixed wild mushrooms (such as girolles, ceps, blewits, morels and shemigi)

sea salt and freshly ground black pepper

To cook:

olive oil

600ml Vegetable Nage (page 211), plus extra for reheating

a little butter

1 teaspoon vitamin C powder, or juice of 1 lemon

Thyme Velouté (page 212)

vegetables à la grecque

This is simply a selection of my favourite vegetables, blanched or lightly fried, then cooled in a balsamic dressing. It's very versatile – serve as a starter, as an accompaniment to grilled steaks or chops, or as a vegetarian main meal for two. **SERVES 4 AS A STARTER OR ACCOMPANIMENT, 2 AS A MAIN COURSE**

2 medium salsify, trimmed

juice of ½ lemon

2 globe artichokes

100g mangetout, trimmed

3 tablespoons olive oil

2 medium carrots, thinly sliced

1 large or 3 small shallots, sliced

2 baby leeks, chopped

1 teaspoon coriander seeds, crushed

3 tablespoons Vinaigrette (page 218)

2 tablespoons balsamic vinegar

1 tablespoon chopped coriander
   leaves

sea salt and freshly ground black
   pepper

1 Peel the salsify thinly, then cut into small batons (or thick julienne strips) and place in a bowl of cold water acidulated with the lemon juice.

2 Prepare the artichokes – only the hearts are used. To expose them, cut off the stalks and pull off all the leaves until you reach the hairy choke. Using a small sharp knife, peel around the base of the heart. Then turn the heart on its side and, using a heavy cook's knife, cut straight down above the heart to remove the hairy fibres of the choke. Scrape off any stray choke with a teaspoon to leave the heart. Cut the artichoke hearts into batons and add to the acidulated water. Halve the mangetout crossways.

3 Bring a large pan of salted water to the boil. Add the salsify and artichoke batons and boil for 2–3 minutes until just tender, but still retaining a good bite. Remove with a slotted spoon and plunge into a bowl of iced water to cool.

4 Add the mangetout to the boiling water and blanch for 1 minute, then drain and add to the iced water to refresh. Drain the cooled vegetables and shake dry.

5 Heat the olive oil in a large frying pan and sauté the carrots, shallot and leeks with the crushed coriander for 2–3 minutes until just softened.

6 Stir in the blanched vegetables and heat for a minute or so. Add the vinaigrette, stir for a few seconds, then finally drizzle the balsamic vinegar over the vegetables. Check the seasoning and serve sprinkled with chopped coriander.

SALSIFY This ugly vegetable doesn't look particularly inviting but it has a good flavour. Peel away the dark outer skin to reveal a pale, creamy flesh that resembles white asparagus. As soon as you peel the vegetable, immerse it in acidulated water (with lemon juice or vitamin C added), otherwise it will turn brown.

fricassée of wild mushrooms

Wild mushrooms have distinctive individual flavours that shine through in this incredibly easy, elegant accompaniment. Make your selection according to the season and the best looking varieties on sale. Don't miss out on my favourite Scottish girolles. Available during the summer, their warm golden glow and flavour add a special quality to this dish. Of course, autumn is prime time for wild mushrooms and our suppliers bring in wonderful ceps, trompettes des morts and blewits at this time of year. Fresh wild mushrooms often contain grit and debris, so you need to wash and dry them carefully before cooking.

SERVES 4 AS AN ACCOMPANIMENT

1 First pick over the wild mushrooms and trim the ends. Slice larger ones if necessary. Soak for a few minutes in a bowl of tepid water, swishing with your hands so all forest debris sinks to the bottom. Drain and shake well, then pat dry in a large clean tea towel or kitchen paper. If not using immediately, spread the mushrooms out on a tray and place them uncovered in the fridge to dry out further.

2 Heat the olive oil in a large frying pan, add the shallot and sauté gently for 3 minutes until softened.

3 Add the butter and when it has melted and starts to foam, toss in the cleaned mushrooms. Sauté for about 5 minutes until they are softened. Season to taste, then mix in the cream and cook for a minute or so.

4 Serve as an accompaniment to grilled meats and fish.

300g selection of wild mushrooms
  (such as ceps, girolles, blewits)
2 tablespoons olive oil
1 shallot, finely chopped
25g butter
100ml double cream
sea salt and freshly ground black
  pepper

CHEF'S TIP Wild mushrooms can be expensive but you can make a delicious fricassée with a combination of fresh wild mushrooms and cultivated brown or chestnut mushrooms. Alternatively, you could use half cultivated mushrooms with just one wild variety, adding some soaked dried porcini or ceps to beef up the flavour.

gratin of Swiss chard with lemon

Swiss chard, or blette as it is called in France, has pale green, thick, fleshy stalks topped with crisp dark green leaves. As the stalks and leaves take different times to cook, they are best cooked separately. Swiss chard is often used to make a creamy tart, but here I've turned it into a tasty gratin. Serve as a vegetarian main course, or accompaniment to simple grilled or roasted meat and fish. **SERVES 4 AS AN ACCOMPANIMENT, 2 AS A MAIN COURSE**

500g Swiss chard leaves

300ml milk

75g butter

20g plain flour

50g grated hard cheese (such as Gruyère, Cheddar or Beaufort)

1 onion, thinly sliced

1 tablespoon olive oil

grated zest of 1 lemon

2 egg yolks

100ml double cream

2 tablespoons freshly grated Parmesan cheese

sea salt and freshly ground black pepper

CHEF'S TIP Swiss chard stalks take longer to cook than the leaves, so they are best treated separately to maximise their flavour and different textures. The stalks need to be blanched first (as you would cook celery); the leaves are then wilted in a similar fashion to spinach.

1 Preheat the oven to 190°C, Gas 5. Wash the chard well and cut the pale green stalks from the leaves with a V-shaped cut at the point where they join. If necessary, peel the stalks lightly, using a swivel peeler, then halve lengthways. Slice the stalks into batons, 1cm thick. Cut the leaves into 2cm thick shreds.

2 Bring a large pan of lightly salted water to the boil. Have ready a large bowl of iced water. Blanch the chard stalk batons in the boiling water for 5 minutes, then remove with a slotted spoon and add to the iced water. Leave for 2–3 minutes, then remove with the slotted spoon and drain.

3 Add the shredded chard to the boiling water and blanch for just over 1 minute. Drain and refresh in the iced water (as above). When cold, remove and drain well, then pat dry with kitchen paper and set aside.

4 To make the sauce, heat the milk in a pan almost until boiling, then remove and set aside. Heat 50g butter in a saucepan until foaming. Stir in the flour and cook, stirring, for 1 minute, then gradually whisk in the hot milk. Cook, stirring constantly, until you have a smooth, glossy sauce with a coating consistency. Simmer for 2 minutes, season to taste and remove from the heat. Stir in the cheese until melted and set aside to cool for 10 minutes.

5 Meanwhile, heat the remaining butter with the olive oil in a frying pan and gently sauté the onion for about 10 minutes until soft and golden. Add the lemon zest and sauté for a few seconds longer. Mix with the chard batons and leaves, then tip into a shallow ovenproof dish.

6 Beat the egg yolks into the cheese sauce. Lightly whip the cream, then fold in. Check the seasoning. Pour the sauce over the chard and onions, stirring gently to combine, then sprinkle with the grated Parmesan. (The dish can be prepared to this point in advance and chilled until ready to serve.)

7 Bake the gratin in the oven for 15 minutes or until golden brown on top, thoroughly hot and bubbling. Leave to stand for 10 minutes before serving.

salad of roasted baby beets with balsamic dressing

Sweet, tender baby beetroot have a wonderful earthy taste. Cook them my way to bring out their full flavour – bake whole (unpeeled) on a bed of rock salt in a foil parcel, then peel, sauté in butter to glaze and dress in good aged balsamic vinegar. I serve the baby beets warm or at room temperature with lamb or oily fish, such as salmon or mackerel. (Illustrated overleaf)

SERVES 4 AS AN ACCOMPANIMENT

1 Preheat the oven to 180°C, Gas 4. Wash the baby beetroot and trim the tops, leaving on a little of the leafy stalks and roots. Pat dry.

2 Lay a large sheet of foil on a baking sheet and spread the rock salt in the centre. Nestle the beetroot in the rock salt and scatter with thyme, tearing the stems into smaller sprigs. Scrunch the foil and bring the edges together to enclose the beetroot and seal.

3 Bake in the oven for about 15–20 minutes until the baby beets are tender. Remove, uncover and leave to cool slightly. Wearing a pair of thin rubber gloves (to avoid staining your hands), peel the beetroot while they are still warm, using a thin-bladed knife. Cut each beetroot in half vertically.

4 Heat the butter in a sauté pan. When it starts to foam, toss in the beetroot and cook, turning frequently, for a couple of minutes until coated in butter and glossy. Add the balsamic vinegar to deglaze and bubble until reduced and syrupy. Serve warm, or at room temperature.

500g baby beetroot
200g rock salt
2–3 thyme sprigs
50g butter
3–4 tablespoons balsamic vinegar

CHEF'S TIP If baby beetroot are unavailable, buy the smallest fresh beetroot you can find and increase the baking time accordingly. After peeling, cut the beetroot into 1cm thick slices before glazing.

CHEF'S SECRET Baking beetroot in their skins on a bed of salt is a great way to draw out some of the moisture, to concentrate and intensify the flavour of the vegetable. The skin protects the beetroot flesh and prevents it becoming salty. As you peel away the skin after baking, you'll simply remove any traces of rock salt, leaving sweet, juicy beets.

fondant of globe artichokes

This classic cooking method gives you lovely tender artichoke hearts to serve warm with melted butter, Vinaigrette (page 218) or Mayonnaise (page 219). When you buy globe artichokes make sure the leaves are plump and glossy, not shrivelled in any way. **SERVES 4 AS A STARTER OR ACCOMPANIMENT**

2 teaspoons vitamin C powder
 (see below)
4 large globe artichokes
1 thyme sprig
1 bay leaf
1 fat garlic clove, halved
10 white peppercorns
10 coriander seeds
1 teaspoon sea salt
4 tablespoons olive oil

1 Dissolve 1 teaspoon vitamin C powder in a large bowl of ice cold water. Snap off the stalks of the artichokes, then pull off all the leaves, until you reach the purple-cream inner leaves. Using a small sharp knife, peel around the base of the heart and trim away the inner leaves. Turn the artichoke on its side and, using a large cook's knife, cut straight across just above the meaty heart to remove the spiky choke. Scrape off any stray wisps of choke with a teaspoon. As you prepare the artichoke hearts, drop them straight into the bowl of acidulated water.

2 When all the artichoke hearts are ready, find a pan that is large enough to take them in a single layer. Cut a circle of greaseproof paper slightly larger than the diameter of the pan to make a cartouche.

3 Remove the artichoke hearts from the cold water and add them to the pan with the herbs, garlic, peppercorns, coriander seeds and salt. Trickle over the olive oil and pour in enough cold water to just cover the hearts. Stir in the remaining vitamin C powder.

4 Press the cartouche on top so that it fits snugly to the side of the pan. Bring to the boil, then lower the heat and simmer for about 20 minutes. To test, insert a skewer into the centre of one artichoke heart – it should meet with little resistance. Remove from the heat and leave the artichokes in the water until ready to serve.

CHEF'S TIP We use vitamin C powder (ascorbic acid) to acidulate water for refreshing vegetables like artichokes that would otherwise quickly oxidise and turn brown. You can buy it in small tubs from pharmacists and some Asian food stores. The good thing about vitamin C powder is that it doesn't affect the delicate flavour of artichokes. If you do not have any, acidulate the water with the juice of 1 lemon instead.

purée of cauliflower scented with herbs

Cauliflower is a versatile vegetable, but it does emit a rather unpleasant aroma when you cook it in the usual way. To counter this, I simmer the florets in milk with added herbs. You can strain off the milk and use it to make a béchamel sauce (see below), serving the florets as a simple accompaniment, or take the dish a stage further as I have here, cooking the cauliflower until really tender then blending to a velvety smooth purée. This purée makes a wonderful base for curry dusted pan-fried fish or scallops.

SERVES 6 AS AN ACCOMPANIMENT

1 Trim the cauliflower, discarding the leaves, and cut into florets. Place in a saucepan and add the milk, herbs and about ½ teaspoon salt. Bring to the boil, then cover and simmer gently. (To serve the florets whole as a simple accompaniment, drain after 5–7 minutes.) For a purée, cook for 12–15 minutes until the cauliflower is very tender.

2 Drain the cauliflower and discard the herbs, reserving the milk. Tip the florets into a blender or food processor. Whiz until very smooth, adding enough of the reserved milk to give a very creamy consistency, scraping down the sides a couple of times. You may need to blend the mixture for up to 5 minutes to achieve a really smooth, silky texture.

3 Taste and adjust the seasoning, adding a little pepper if required. Serve piping hot.

1 medium cauliflower

300ml milk

1 small bay leaf

1 thyme sprig

sea salt and freshly ground white
  pepper

COOK'S TIP The milk in which the cauliflower is cooked can be used to flavour a béchamel. Make the roux in the usual way, then incorporate the flavoured milk and cook, stirring, until smooth.

fondue of Little Gem lettuce

If you have never eaten cooked lettuce, I urge you to try it! Cooked in light, buttery stock, this salad vegetable is surprisingly delicious and makes an excellent accompaniment to poultry and fish. And because it is tender and creamy, you won't need to make a special sauce or gravy to go with the meal. Little Gem lettuce, with their tightly packed leaves, are the best choice here – allow one per person.

SERVES 4 AS AN ACCOMPANIMENT

4 Little Gem lettuces
2 tablespoons olive oil
75g butter, in cubes
200ml Chicken Stock (page 210)
1 thyme sprig
sea salt and freshly ground black
  pepper

1 Cut the lettuces in half lengthways, but don't cut off the stalks. Carefully wash and pat dry with kitchen paper.

2 Heat the olive oil in a sauté pan. When it is really hot, lay the lettuce halves in the pan, cut-side down. Season and cook over a medium heat for about 2 minutes until lightly caramelised.

3 Gradually add the butter in pieces and the stock, then scatter in the thyme, torn into tiny sprigs. Cover the lettuce with a butter paper or a scrunched sheet of wet greaseproof paper. Cook on a low heat for about 8 minutes, basting once or twice, until the lettuce is tender but still holds its shape. The liquid should have reduced to a glossy glaze by now. Allow to stand for 5 minutes before serving.

CHEF'S TIP Frying the lettuce halves first in hot olive oil caramelises the outer leaves and gives them a succulent, sweet flavour. Braising them in light stock with butter thereafter enhances the flavour and lends a creamy texture.

braised spiced red cabbage with juniper

The simplest cooking techniques are often the best. Here, red cabbage is cooked long and slow, yet obligingly retains its texture and colour. It can even be made ahead and reheated without loss of flavour. Don't be tempted to use the more refined wine vinegar, for this dish malt vinegar lends the appropriate flavour. However, the amount of sugar and butter can be adjusted to taste – I prefer mine sweet and buttery. This dish is wonderful with roast pork, duck, goose and the Christmas turkey.

SERVES 6–8 AS AN ACCOMPANIMENT

1 red cabbage, about 500g

250ml malt vinegar

100g demerara sugar

125g butter, diced

1 teaspoon sea salt

2 star anise

½ teaspoon coriander seeds

10 juniper berries

freshly ground black pepper

1 Preheat the oven to 140°C, Gas 1. Quarter the cabbage and cut out the core. Pull off any outer leaves that are damaged or wilted, then shred each cabbage quarter as finely as possible, using a sharp knife or mandolin.

2 Place the cabbage in a large cast-iron casserole. Add the vinegar, sugar, butter and salt. Tie the star anise, coriander seeds and juniper berries in a small square of muslin and nestle in the centre of the cabbage.

3 Cover the casserole. A good seal is essential, so if the lid isn't tight-fitting, cover the casserole with foil, then put the lid on. Cook for up to 3 hours, until the cabbage is tender, giving it a good stir halfway through cooking.

4 When the cabbage is tender, check to see if any juices remain. If so, strain them into a pan and boil down to reduce until syrupy, then stir back into the casserole. Discard the bag of spices and adjust the seasoning before serving.

JUNIPER BERRIES These dark blue berries have a sweet, aromatic flavour, reminiscent of pine. They have a natural affinity with cabbage, and are often used to flavour rich meat and game dishes.

celeriac 'lasagne'

Celeriac may not be the most attractive vegetable, but it has a good flavour. Here I've cooked it in two ways – sliced and as a purée, then combined the two to make an original accompaniment. Serve with meat or fish, or try the varation and serve as a light main meal. The dish can be prepared ahead and reheated without spoiling. **SERVES 4 AS AN ACCOMPANIMENT**

1 Preheat the oven to 190°C, Gas 5. Cut the top and base from the celeriac, then peel away the skin with a swivel peeler – you'll find it easier to work around the circumference of the vegetable than peel from top to bottom. Trim away the knobbly root ends.

2 Stand the celeriac on a board, on its flat base, and cut down the middle into two halves. Cut four large, 5mm thick rounds from each half and place in a bowl of cold water acidulated with half of the lemon juice.

3 Chop the rest of the celeriac into small, even dice. Add to a pan of boiling salted water with the remaining lemon juice and bring back to the boil. Cook for about 15 minutes until just tender. Remove with a slotted spoon and transfer to a blender or food processor.

4 Return the water to the boil. Using a slotted spoon, lift the celeriac rounds from the acidulated water and slide into the boiling water. Simmer for 10–12 minutes until just tender and still holding a good shape. Drain the slices carefully so they stay intact. Set aside.

5 Meanwhile, whiz the diced celeriac until smooth, adding the butter and cream, to give a very creamy textured purée. Adjust the seasoning.

6 Spread half the celeriac purée over the base of a shallow ovenproof dish and cover with half the celeriac slices. Repeat these layers, then sprinkle the grated Parmesan over the surface. (The dish can be prepared to this point in advance and chilled until ready to serve.)

7 To serve, bake in the oven for about 15 minutes or until golden brown on top, thoroughly hot and bubbling. Leave to stand for 5 minutes before serving.

VARIATION
Stir-fry 250g peeled tiger prawns until tender, dust with curry powder and toss in lime or lemon juice. Slice the prawns in half lengthways, then layer half on each layer of celeriac purée. Finish as above. Serve as a light meal.

1 large celeriac, about 750g
juice of 1 lemon
60g butter, softened
4 tablespoons double cream
2 tablespoons freshly grated
  Parmesan cheese
sea salt and freshly ground black
  pepper

sautéed broccoli with crispy garlic and oyster sauce

Broccoli is a highly versatile vegetable and very popular, but it is so easily overcooked. One minute it is too hard, the next it is unpalatably limp and watery. My solution is to blanch the florets briefly in boiling water, then immediately refresh them in iced water. When ready to serve, I stir-fry the broccoli quickly; here it is served Chinese style with a contrast of crispy garlic slivers. An ideal accompaniment for fish or chicken. **SERVES 4 AS AN ACCOMPANIMENT**

1 large head of broccoli, about 500g

2 tablespoons sunflower or olive oil

2 fat garlic cloves, thinly sliced

1 tablespoon sesame oil

1 onion, thinly sliced

2 tablespoons oyster sauce

sea salt and freshly ground black
  pepper

1 Cut off the main stalk, then cut the broccoli into small florets. Have ready a large bowl of iced water.

2 Bring a large pan of salted water to the boil, add the broccoli florets and blanch for 2 minutes, timing from the moment the water returns to the boil. Immediately drain the broccoli and tip into the bowl of iced water to refresh. Drain and set aside until ready to serve.

3 Heat 1 tablespoon sunflower or olive oil in a frying pan. When it is hot, add the garlic slivers and sauté until golden brown and crispy. Do not allow to scorch or the garlic will taste bitter. Immediately remove with a slotted spoon and drain on kitchen paper.

4 When ready to serve, heat the remaining sunflower or olive oil in the pan, together with the sesame oil. Add the onion slices and sauté over a medium heat for about 5 minutes until softened.

5 Add the broccoli florets and sauté until piping hot, tossing carefully to ensure the florets are not broken up. Mix in the oyster sauce, then add the crisp garlic slivers. Adjust the seasoning and serve immediately.

REFRESHING This is an important technique that helps to preserve the vibrant colour and freshness of vegetables, by preventing them overcooking. It's especially useful for fast-cooking green vegetables like broccoli. All you need is plenty of iced water to hand – add 3 good handfuls of ice cubes to a large bowl of cold water. As soon as you drain the vegetables from the boiling water, immediately plunge them into the iced water. Leave for about 5 minutes to cool thoroughly, then drain the vegetables and set aside, ready to reheat and serve. The water can be used again, simply replenish the ice cubes.

CHEF'S TIP Blanching baby onions in boiling water for 30 seconds to 1 minute will loosen their skins and make it much easier to peel them. However, for this dish, you will find that the onions won't caramelise as successfully if they have been pre-blanched, so avoid doing so unless you are very short of time.

caramelised baby onions with beetroot jus

Here baby onions, or shallots, are cooked in a beetroot jus until they take on a rich magenta glaze, then served as an accompaniment in their own right, rather than used merely as a flavouring ingredient. Make your own jus if you have a juicer, using raw beetroot, or buy bottled beetroot juice from a healthfood shop. **SERVES 4–6 AS AN ACCOMPANIMENT**

1 If using fresh beetroot, peel them, wearing thin rubber gloves to stop your fingers staining. Chop roughly and whiz through your juicer. If using bottled beetroot juice, strain and pass through a fine sieve so the liquid is clear. You need about 200ml juice.

2 Heat the butter in a large sauté pan. When it starts to foam, add the whole baby onions or shallots, with the thyme and sugar, and cook for about 5 minutes until lightly caramelised. Season with salt and pepper as they cook.

3 Pour in the beetroot juice and stock or vegetable nage. Bring to the boil, then cook uncovered for a further 5 minutes, stirring occasionally, until the onions are just tender; they should still retain a bite. Using a slotted spoon, transfer the onions to a dish.

4 Bubble up the pan juices until reduced to a syrupy glaze. Return the onions to the pan and heat through, turning to coat in the glaze. Discard the thyme.

1 large fresh beetroot (about 250g) or
   200ml bottled beetroot juice
100g butter
250g baby onions or small shallots,
   peeled
few thyme sprigs
½ teaspoon sugar
100ml Chicken Stock (page 210) or
   Vegetable Nage (page 211)
sea salt and freshly ground black
   pepper

parsnip crisps

Beyond potatoes, I think parsnips make the best deep-fried crisps. To create wafer-thin broad ribbons, buy maincrop rather than young parsnips, you'll also need a swivel vegetable peeler. A light dusting of curry salt makes them irresistible, but you may prefer to omit this if serving the crisps as an accompaniment rather than a snack. They go particularly well with venison, beef steaks and game birds. **SERVES 4 AS AN ACCOMPANIMENT**

4 medium parsnips
vegetable oil for deep-frying,
  about 500ml
about 1 teaspoon curry salt
  (see right)

1 Peel the parsnips, then top and tail them. Using a swivel vegetable peeler, mandolin or Japanese vegetable slicer, shave each parsnip lengthways into wafer-thin slices.

2 Pour the oil into a deep-fat fryer or deep, heavy saucepan; it should one-third fill the pan. Heat the oil until it registers 180°C on a frying thermometer, or until a small cube of day-old bread dropped into the oil browns in 30 seconds.

3 Deep-fry the parsnip wafers, a handful at a time. Using a slotted spoon, add them to the oil and deep-fry for 2–3 minutes until golden brown and crisp. As they fry, keep moving the parsnip crisps around in the pan with the back of the spoon to ensure an even colour.

4 Remove and drain on kitchen paper, then immediately sprinkle the crisps with the curry salt while they are still piping hot, so the flavour is readily absorbed. Keep warm in a low oven, uncovered, while you cook the remaining crisps. Return the oil to the correct temperature in between frying each batch.

5 Serve the parsnip crisps as soon as you have cooked them all.

CURRY SALT This has so many uses, it's worth making more than you need and storing the rest in a small jar. I sprinkle it on to scallops, prawns, fish and chicken, to enhance their flavour. To prepare, simply mix 1 teaspoon medium curry powder to every 2 teaspoons fine sea salt.

pomme purée

There are three secrets to a velvety smooth pomme purée. The first is the choice of potato. You need one with a good flavour and floury texture, such as Desirée or King Edward. Then, to make sure the potato cooks evenly, cut it into chunks of the same size. Finally, press the potato through a mouli or potato ricer, rather than mash or beat it, to achieve a silky, even texture. To keep it light, add hot cream and beat in diced butter. Serve plain, or try one of my suggested flavourings below.

SERVES 4–6 AS AN ACCOMPANIMENT

1kg floury potatoes (such as Desirée or King Edward)
150ml double cream
60–90g butter, cut into small cubes
sea salt and freshly ground black pepper

1 Peel the potatoes thinly, then cut in even-sized chunks, about 5cm. Add to a pan of lightly salted water and bring to the boil. Simmer until tender, allowing about 15 minutes from the moment the water returns to the boil, but check after 12 minutes.

2 Drain the potatoes, then return to the pan over the heat to dry out for a few minutes. Then pass the potatoes through a vegetable mouli or press through a potato ricer.

3 Meanwhile, boil the cream in a small pan until reduced by half. Stir into the potatoes and season with salt and pepper to taste. Now, gradually work in the cubes of butter, according to how rich you want the purée to be. A good pomme purée will be able to take a lot of butter without 'splitting'. Keep warm or chill until required and reheat in a pan or microwave to serve.

FLAVOURINGS
Horseradish Add 2–3 tablespoons horseradish relish to the finished purée.
Mustard Add 1 tablespoon coarse grain mustard and 1 teaspoon horseradish relish to the finished purée.
Truffle Add a few drops of truffle oil to the finished purée. Serve sprinkled with a little very finely chopped black truffle if available.
Celeriac Peel and chop ½ small celeriac, about 250g, and boil in lightly salted water until tender. Drain and whiz in a blender or food processor until velvety smooth. Mix into the pomme purée with the cream and seasoning.
Basil Heat 4 large basil leaves in the cream as you reduce it to infuse. Remove the basil before mixing into the pomme purée.

pommes dauphinoise

For this creamy potato gratin, you need to buy a waxy variety that will retain its texture as it absorbs liquid. A traditional gratin is cooked entirely in the oven, but I prefer to simmer the potatoes first in milk on the hob, then finish the dish in the oven. This method cuts the cooking time and gives you a more dependable result. The potatoes should be of a similar size.

SERVES 4 AS AN ACCOMPANIMENT

1 Preheat the oven to 200°C, Gas 6. Peel the potatoes thinly, then slice evenly into 1cm slices. Bring the milk and cream to the boil in a large saucepan and add the garlic, herbs and seasoning. Simmer for a couple of minutes.

2 Slide the potatoes into the pan and stir gently. Simmer for about 7 minutes until the potato slices are only just tender; they should hold their shape and retain a bite. Drain the par-cooked potatoes in a colander set over a bowl to catch the creamy milk.

3 Layer the potatoes in a shallow ovenproof dish, sprinkling two thirds of the cheese and seasoning in between the layers. Trickle a little of the saved milk over each layer too.

4 Pour a little more of the milk around the sides, but not too much – just enough to moisten. Sprinkle over the last of the cheese.

5 Place the dish in a shallow roasting tin and bake for about 10–15 minutes or until the cheese is beginning to bubble and turn golden brown. Allow to stand for 10 minutes before serving.

600g slightly waxy potatoes (such as
   La Ratte or Maris Piper)
350ml milk
350ml double cream
1 large garlic clove, sliced
1 thyme sprig
1 bay leaf
90g Gruyère cheese, grated
sea salt and freshly ground black
   pepper

CHEF'S TIP Making sure the potatoes are just cooked before you layer them takes the guess work out of this classic baked potato dish and ensures that it is always creamy with a nice bite.

Eggs

Where would we be without eggs? The versatility of this indispensable ingredient never ceases to amaze me – a food scientist's dream. Not only do eggs thicken and enrich sauces, bind stuffings, lighten and expand on whisking to create soufflés and meringues, they can also be cooked in a variety of ways to serve as a meal in their own right. I even have fond memories of the 'egg sarnies' my mother packed into my lunch box for school outings. No one sat next to me because of the smell, but I didn't care – they tasted great.

Our eggs are always free-range because the flavour is better. A couple of fresh eggs, a knob of butter and a handful of chopped herbs and you always have a meal. Or in the case of le Gavroche, a couple of the finest fresh eggs scrambled slowly with butter, piled on to toasted Polâine bread, topped with sliced ceps and served with a fresh tomato purée and torn basil leaves.

And recently I have discovered the delights of duck eggs. Not only are the yolks naturally brighter yellow and larger than hens' eggs, but the whites also have a superior flavour. Duck eggs are fabulous with fresh asparagus and they make the best cakes. Goose eggs are also great in cakes, though like rare gulls' eggs, they are seasonal. Quails' eggs are farmed and sold all year round.

One word of warning, if you think you might have a reaction to lightly cooked eggs, then avoid recipes that use raw or lightly set eggs. We use the freshest eggs possible from quality farmers and recommend you do the same.

eggs benedict with minted hollandaise

In 1894 a Wall Street broker, Lemuel Benedict, ordered the chef at New York's Waldorf Hotel to put together all his favourite foods – eggs, bacon, toast and Hollandaise – to cure a hangover. A century on, with muffins instead of toast and a minted hollandaise, this is still one of our popular breakfast dishes at Claridges. We poach the eggs ahead and keep the hollandaise warm in a bain marie, because it cannot be reheated once it has cooled and solidified. **SERVES 4 AS A LIGHT MEAL**

4 large free-range eggs
knob of butter
2 muffins, split
4–8 slices Parma ham

Minted hollandaise:
150g unsalted butter
2 free-range egg yolks
6 coriander seeds, crushed
1½ teaspoons reduced white wine
   vinegar (see below)
squeeze of lemon juice
pinch of cayenne pepper
4 large mint leaves, cut into thin
   julienne strips
sea salt

1 To make the hollandaise, melt the butter in a pan over a gentle heat, then carefully pour off the golden oil into a jug and discard the milky solids. Set the clarified butter aside to cool until lukewarm.

2 Put the egg yolks, crushed coriander and 1 tablespoon cold water into a heatproof bowl and fit snugly over a pan of gently simmering water. Using a hand-held stick blender or electric whisk, beat until very light and frothy (this makes it easier to incorporate the butter).

3 Remove the bowl from the heat and continue whisking for a couple more minutes, then slowly trickle in the runny butter as you continue to whisk. Don't add the butter too quickly or it will curdle. When all the butter is incorporated, season with salt and add the reduced vinegar, lemon juice and cayenne. Finally, fold in the chopped mint. Set the bowl back over the pan of hot water (but off the heat) to keep warm; stir occasionally to stop a skin forming. If the sauce does happen to split, whisk in a trickle of cold water to re-emulsify it.

4 Poach the eggs: you can do this in advance for convenience, and to avoid overcooking them (see below).

5 To assemble, toast the split muffins lightly on both sides. If you have poached the eggs ahead, using a slotted spoon, transfer them to a pan containing enough boiling hot buttery water to cover. Leave to stand off the heat for 15–20 seconds, no longer or the yolks won't be soft. Remove with a slotted spoon and drain well.

6 Butter the muffins and place on warmed plates. Arrange 1 or 2 slices of Parma ham on each muffin, sit a poached egg on top and finally coat with the warm hollandaise. Serve immediately.

REDUCED WINE VINEGAR It's useful to keep a small bottle of this in the fridge. To prepare, pour 250ml white wine vinegar into a pan, add ½ small shallot, sliced, a blade of mace and ¼ teaspoon black peppercorns. Boil until reduced by half, then strain through a sieve, cool and pour into a small bottle.

POACHING EGGS TO PERFECTION It is absolutely essential to use very fresh eggs to ensure the whites hold together. Half-fill a shallow saucepan with water, add a dash of vinegar and bring to a steady simmer. Meanwhile, break an egg into a cup. To help the egg set to a neat shape, lightly whisk the water, using a slow circular movement, then reduce the heat to a low simmer. Slide the egg into the pan and poach for 1½ minutes. Carefully lift out and place in a bowl of chilled water to stop the cooking. Repeat with the remaining eggs and refrigerate until needed.

fried duck eggs with griddled asparagus

Free-range duck eggs are becoming much more widely available, which is terrific. They're about 25% larger than a hen's egg with a bright yellow, rich, creamy yolk that stands proud of the white. They are superb fried, but the frying must be gentle, almost as a confit technique, so the egg white sets without crisping. Ideally, you need two blini pans, about 12cm in diameter. Otherwise use the smallest frying pan you have in the kitchen. This is a great dish to cook when homegrown asparagus starts to appear in shops and markets, around late spring. **SERVES 2 AS A LIGHT MEAL**

200g green asparagus spears

good olive oil, to drizzle and fry

40g butter, cut into thin flakes

2 free-range duck eggs, or extra large
  hen's eggs

about 30g Parmesan cheese, finely
  pared into shavings

handful of rocket leaves, about 25g

sea salt and freshly coarse ground
  black pepper

1 Peel the lower stems of the asparagus, using a swivel peeler. Bring a pan of lightly salted water to the boil and blanch the spears for 1 minute. Drain and refresh in a bowl of ice-cold water for 5 minutes, then drain and pat dry. Place the blanched asparagus in a shallow dish, drizzle with olive oil and turn to coat.

2 Pour 1 tablespoon olive oil into each of two 12cm blini pans, add a small knob of butter and place over a medium heat. When you can feel a gentle heat rising, crack a duck egg into each pan and fry gently until cooked to perfection (see below). Duck eggs will take 8–10 minutes; hen's eggs 5–6 minutes.

3 In the meantime, heat a griddle pan over a high heat until you can feel a good heat rising, then add the asparagus spears and cook for about 2–3 minutes, turning occasionally, until tender and lightly charred.

4 To serve, arrange the asparagus on two warmed large plates and season. Scatter over the Parmesan shavings and rocket leaves, dressing these very lightly with olive oil if you like. Carefully place a fried egg on top, coarsely grind over some pepper and serve straightaway.

PERFECT FRIED EGGS

Crack the egg into the hot oiled pan over a medium heat. Tilt the pan to centre the yolk – it will set in position after about 30 seconds. Lower the heat and cook until the egg white starts to firm, about 4 minutes for duck eggs, 3 minutes for extra large hen's eggs. Slip the butter flakes down the side of the pan. As the butter begins to foam, spoon it over the egg whites to help them cook. Season lightly and cook until the whites are just set firm and the yolks are still soft and runny. Loosen the edge with a small palette knife and remove.

tartlets of scrambled eggs with smoked salmon

Scrambled eggs, and the way they are cooked, is a matter of personal taste. I like them creamy and fine-textured, achieved by preparing them in the classic way. For an elegant light meal, I line crisp pastry tartlets with smoked salmon, fill them with warm scrambled eggs and top with a little caviar – Osietra is my preferred choice. For a less extravagant finish, you can simply top with smoked salmon strips and snipped chives. To treat the palate to an unforgettable experience, serve the caviar-topped tartlets with a swirl of reduced lobster bisque. **SERVES 4 AS A STARTER OR LIGHT MEAL**

1 First, make the tartlet cases. Cut the pastry into four, then roll out each portion thinly to a round and use to line four 10cm tartlet tins with removable bases. Bring the pastry high up the sides, so it protrudes about 1cm above the rim. Prick the bases with a fork. Then carefully stack the pastry-lined tins, one on top of the other – this helps keeps the pastry thin and crisp as it cooks. Line the exposed top tartlet with foil and baking beans. Leave the stack of tart cases to rest in the fridge for 15 minutes.

2 Preheat the oven to 200°C, Gas 6. Place the tartlet cases, still in a stack, on a heavy baking sheet and bake for about 15 minutes until golden brown. Remove the foil and baking beans, and carefully separate the tartlet tins. Trim the pastry edges level with the rim of the tins, using a sharp knife. Return to the oven for 3–5 minutes to crisp the pastry.

3 In the meantime, if serving lobster bisque, boil to reduce by half; keep warm.

4 When ready to serve, make the scrambled eggs. Put the butter into a wide, shallow pan over a low heat. As it begins to melt, add the eggs and whisk vigorously with a balloon whisk as they start to heat. When the eggs begin to scramble, pour in the cream and milk. Immediately remove from the heat, season and stir gently with a fork until creamy.

5 Remove the tartlet cases from the tins. Line the sides with the smoked salmon, so it extends high above the rims. Place on warmed serving plates and fill with the warm scrambled eggs. Top with a spoonful of caviar and surround each tartlet with a drizzle of reduced lobster bisque if you like. Alternatively, simply top with a few smoked salmon strips and snipped chives. Serve immediately.

350g Puff Pastry (page 190), or
   ready-made puff
40g butter, diced
6 large or 8 medium free-range eggs
4 tablespoons double cream
4 tablespoons milk
150g sliced smoked salmon
sea salt and freshly ground black
   pepper

To serve:
200ml Lobster Bisque (page 12,
   optional)
4 teaspoons caviar
or extra strips of smoked salmon and
   snipped chives

CLASSIC SCRAMBLED EGGS Use a wide, shallow pan set over a medium heat to begin with. Add the butter and as soon as it starts to melt, crack in the eggs. Using a balloon whisk, beat vigorously until the eggs form soft curds, then whisk in the cream and milk. This will slow the cuisson down and achieve the correct creamy texture. Season at this stage, not before, and continue to stir gently until soft and creamy. Serve without delay.

Swiss soufflés

These impressive, delicate béchamel soufflés are cooked in individual ramekins, then turned out to finish cooking in a gratin dish of cream, with a generous sprinkling of Gruyère. Like all soufflés, they need to be served the moment they are ready, so have warmed serving plates – and your guests – ready and waiting. **SERVES 4 AS A STARTER OR LIGHT MEAL**

300ml milk

1 bay leaf

½ small onion

30g butter

30g plain flour

25g Parmesan cheese, freshly grated

2 large free-range eggs, separated,
   plus 1 extra egg white

melted butter, to brush

2–3 tablespoons natural colour dried
   breadcrumbs

400ml double cream

freshly grated nutmeg

100g Gruyère or Emmenthal cheese,
   grated

sea salt and freshly ground black
   pepper

1 Put the milk into a pan with the bay leaf and onion and bring to a simmer, then remove from the heat and set aside to infuse for 30 minutes. Discard the bay leaf and onion. Reheat the milk.

2 Melt the butter in a medium saucepan and stir in the flour. Cook, stirring, over a gentle heat for 1–2 minutes. Gradually whisk in the hot milk, to make a smooth sauce. Simmer for 2 minutes, stirring once or twice. Remove from the heat, beat in the Parmesan and season with salt and pepper to taste. Stir in the 2 egg yolks, cover and allow the mixture to cool.

3 When ready to serve, preheat the oven to 200°C, Gas 6 and prepare four ramekins, 9cm in diameter. Brush the insides evenly with melted butter, then sprinkle in the crumbs and tap all round to coat with an even layer, tipping out any excess. Stand the ramekins on a baking sheet.

4 In a clean grease-free bowl, whisk the 3 egg whites with a good pinch of salt until they form soft firm peaks. Beat a third of the egg whites into the sauce to lighten it, then using a large metal spoon, gently fold in the rest. Divide between the ramekins and level the tops. Bake for 10–12 minutes until well risen and the surface is set and golden brown.

5 In the meantime, pour the cream into a large shallow ovenproof gratin dish and sprinkle with salt, pepper and nutmeg.

6 Now work fast! As soon as the soufflés are ready, quickly run a thin table knife round the side of each one. Holding each ramekin with a cloth, upend the soufflés into the cream, one at a time. Sprinkle the grated cheese over the top and bake in the oven for 10 minutes. Serve immediately.

CHEF'S TIP It is important to whisk the egg whites to the correct softly peaking consistency. If over-beaten the whites will become grainy and you won't be able to fold them into the mixture smoothly. The soufflé mixture can be prepared to the end of step 2 well in advance (up to 24 hours) and kept in the fridge until ready to finish and serve.

perfect cheese omelette

In theory it's easy to make an omelette, but the timing is critical. The perfect omelette is pale golden on the outside without the slightest tinge of brown, and soft and creamy in the centre, which the French term bauvese. If overcooked, an omelette will be hard and leathery, and quite unpalatable. The secret lies in the technique of constantly stirring and shaking the pan during cooking, then folding and tipping the omelette straight on to a warmed serving plate so it folds neatly into three.

SERVES 1 AS A LIGHT MEAL

1 Place a 20–21cm omelette pan over a medium-high heat. Beat the eggs in a bowl until evenly blended, but don't add salt or pepper at this stage. Add the olive oil to the pan and, when you can feel a good heat rising, slip in the butter and swirl it in the pan as it foams and melts.

2 Pour in the beaten eggs and swirl them round and round in the pan with a fork, shaking the pan frequently with one hand. The trick is to get the eggs to an even light, creamy texture at this stage.

3 When the mixture is three-quarters set, stop stirring with the fork and leave undisturbed for 30 seconds or so, until the base of the omelette is just set. Loosen the edges with a palette knife.

4 Wrap your free hand in a clean tea towel, hold the pan just off the heat, tilt away from you and bang the side opposite the handle on the surface a few times. This has the effect of shaking the omelette loose from the pan so that it begins to slide on to the edge furthest away from you.

5 At this point, season with salt and pepper and scatter over the cheese. Then, holding the pan handle again, flip the third of the omelette furthest from you into the centre. Now hold the pan over a warmed plate and slide the omelette out, so it folds over into a neat roll. For real perfection, use your tea towel to shape the omelette roll neatly. And that's it. The heat of the creamy centre is sufficient to melt the cheese. Serve at once.

3 medium free-range eggs
1 tablespoon olive oil
large knob of butter, about 15g
50g grated Gruyère or mature
   Cheddar cheese
sea salt and freshly ground black
   pepper

CHEF'S SECRET Don't season the eggs before you cook them, because salt breaks down the albumen in the egg white and thins the mixture, giving a less satisfactory result.

THE RIGHT TOOLS The choice of pan is important. You need a frying pan about 21cm in diameter, with rounded sides that make it easier to flip the omelette. We use a heavy duty non-stick pan that can take metal forks, but if yours is not as robust, then use a wooden or heatproof plastic fork for stirring.

open omelette of goat's cheese and spinach

As a modification of the perfect omelette technique, chunks of chèvre and baby spinach leaves are scattered on top of a soft-set omelette, which is then flashed under the grill to lightly colour the chèvre. I use a cendré (ash-coated) goat's cheese, but you could substitute a herb-coated chèvre if you prefer. Serve straight from the pan with a mixed leaf salad and crusty bread.

SERVES 2 AS A LIGHT MEAL

2 good handfuls of baby spinach
   leaves, about 50g
2 tablespoons olive oil
4 large free-range eggs
20g butter, diced
100g good, soft chèvre (preferably
   cendré), with rind
2 tablespoons freshly grated
   Parmesan cheese
sea salt and freshly ground black
   pepper

1 Preheat the grill to medium. Put the spinach into a saucepan with 1 tablespoon olive oil and place over a low heat for about 30 seconds until lightly wilted, then remove from the heat and drain on kitchen paper. Tease the lightly cooked leaves apart to separate.

2 Place a 21–23cm omelette pan over a medium-high heat. Beat the eggs in a bowl until evenly blended, but don't add salt or pepper. When you can feel a good heat rising, add the remaining tablespoon olive oil to the pan and swirl round the base, then drop in the diced butter and allow to melt and foam.

3 When the butter is foaming, pour in the eggs. Take a fork (ideally metal if your pan will take it, otherwise a wooden or heatproof plastic one) and stir the egg mixture round in the pan. When the mixture is two-thirds set, stop stirring with the fork. Pinch the chèvre into pieces and scatter these and the spinach leaves over the surface of the omelette. Season lightly (you won't need much salt because of the cheese). Sprinkle with the Parmesan.

4 Now place the omelette pan under the grill until the top is lightly set and the cheese is golden. Remove from the heat and loosen the edges with a palette knife. Slide the omelette out of the pan and serve, cut into wedges.

VARIATIONS

Try one of the following alternative toppings:

Caramelised onion and anchovy Cook 2–3 sliced red onions slowly in olive oil with a light sprinkling of sugar until softened and caramelised. Cool slightly, then scatter over the half-set omelette and top with 4–6 snipped anchovy fillets. Finish as above.

Confit of cherry tomatoes Slow roast cherry tomatoes in olive oil with thyme and seasoning until tender. Scatter over the half-set omelette with torn basil. Finish as above.

Omelette Arnold Bennet Top the half-set omelette with flaked, poached smoked haddock, creamy Mornay cheese sauce and grated cheese. Gratiné under the grill as above.

CHEF'S TIP When ready to serve, unmould the parfaits directly on to serving plates. If using metal moulds, briefly wipe a hot cloth around them to loosen the parfaits, then lift the moulds off. If using ramekins, simply lift out the wrapped parfaits and peel away the cling film. Quickly top each parfait with a scoop of ice cream and finish with chocolate shavings. Serve immediately.

chocolate and tiramisu parfait

These decadent parfaits comprise three layers: a chocolate hazelnut base, a sabayon flavoured with fortified wines, and a scoop of vanilla or white chocolate ice cream on top. Use a homemade ice cream (pages 158–9), or buy a good quality luxury brand. To mould the parfaits, use metal cutters if possible (available from good cookshops), or ramekins. As sabayon never freezes solid, the parfaits must be served promptly. **SERVES 6**

1 For the chocolate layer, put the chocolate, hazelnuts, icing sugar, cream and rum into a heatproof bowl. Set over a pan of gently simmering water until the chocolate has melted, stirring occasionally. Remove and stir well until smooth and creamy. Leave to cool to room temperature.

2 Meanwhile, set six 6cm metal ring cutters on a tray lined with cling film. Or line 6 ramekins with cling film, pressing well into the sides and base for a snug fit, and allowing plenty to overhang the sides.

3 Give the chocolate mixture a stir, then spoon into the moulds. Tap on a work surface to level the mixture, then put in the freezer.

4 Now make the sabayon. Put the egg yolks, sugar, Madeira and Marsala into a large heatproof bowl. Set this over a pan of gently simmering water and whisk, using an electric hand whisk or balloon whisk, for at least 10 minutes until you have a pale golden light, stable foam, the consistency of thick double cream. The sabayon is ready when the mixture leaves a trail as the beaters are lifted.

5 Remove from the heat and continue whisking for another 5 minutes or so, until cool. Take the moulds or ramekins from the freezer and spoon the sabayon on top of the chocolate layer. Return to the freezer and freeze until firm.

6 Unmould the parfaits and top with ice cream and chocolate shavings to serve.

Chocolate hazelnut base:
100g good quality milk chocolate (such as Valrhona's Jivara), about 30% cocoa solids
30g roasted chopped hazelnuts
1 tablespoon icing sugar
100ml double cream
1 tablespoon rum

Sabayon:
5 free-range egg yolks
100g caster sugar
1½ tablespoons Madeira or medium dry sherry
1½ tablespoons Marsala

To serve:
6 small scoops White Chocolate Ice Cream (page 159) or Classic Vanilla Ice Cream (page 158)
dark chocolate shavings

CHOCOLATE SHAVINGS
The easiest way to shape thin chocolate curls is to shave them directly from a block of chocolate, using a swivel vegetable peeler or sharp knife. The chocolate must be at room temperature, not taken straight from the fridge.

Eton mess

Originally a tuck shop treat at that well known boarding school, Eton Mess has evolved into a scrumptious pudding that couldn't be easier to prepare. Meringues are simply crushed, then folded into whipped cream with chopped strawberries. Easy French meringue is used here – it bakes to a crispness on the surface, but remains slightly gooey inside. **SERVES 6–8**

Meringue:
2 large free-range egg whites
pinch of fine sea salt or squeeze of
   lemon juice
100g vanilla sugar (see below), or
   caster sugar

To assemble:
400ml double cream
250g ripe strawberries, hulled
2 tablespoons kirsch or sherry
   (optional)
1 tablespoon chopped pistachio nuts
   (unsalted)

1 Preheat the oven to its lowest setting, maximum 100°C, Gas ¼. Line a baking sheet with baking parchment.
2 Place the egg whites in a clean, grease-free bowl. Add the salt or lemon juice and whisk with a hand-held electric whisk until the egg whites just hold firm peaks. Do not over-beat or the mixture will become dry and grainy.
3 Gradually whisk in the sugar, a tablespoonful at a time, until you have a firm glossy meringue that holds its shape.
4 Spread this on the prepared baking sheet in an even layer, about 2cm thick. Bake for at least 2 hours until lightly crusty on top. If your oven is very low, or you are using a warming oven, the meringues may be left inside to dry out for up to 6 hours. Carefully lift the meringue (by the paper) on to a wire rack. Leave to cool completely, then peel off the paper. Break the meringue into 2–3cm pieces.
5 Whip the cream just until it forms soft floppy peaks. Roughly cut up the strawberries and toss with the kirsch or sherry if using.
6 When ready to serve fold the crushed meringues and strawberries into the cream and spoon into 6 or 8 small dishes. Sprinkle with chopped pistachio nuts and serve.

VANILLA SUGAR Make your own fragrant vanilla sugar by burying 1 or 2 vanilla pods in a jar of caster sugar. Leave to infuse for at least 48 hours before using. Keep the pods in the jar and replenish the sugar as necessary.

CHEF'S SECRETS Very fresh eggs are not the secret to successful meringue. The best texture is achieved with eggs that are at least 1 week old. You will also get a better result if the egg whites are at room temperature, rather than taken straight from the fridge. If you have separated egg whites in the fridge destined for meringue, but you're not sure how many, weigh them and use an equal quantity of sugar.

île flottante

This is my version of a favourite French dessert that cleverly illustrates the versatility of eggs. The yolks go to make an espresso coffee crème anglaise, while the whites are whisked up to make meringues, which are gently poached rather than baked. To serve, the billowy meringues are floated on the coffee custard and drizzled with caramel. **SERVES 4**

1 First make the custard. Put the egg yolks and brown sugar into a heatproof bowl and whisk until thick and creamy. Meanwhile, bring the cream and milk almost to the boil in a heavy-based pan and stir in the coffee. Slowly pour the creamy coffee milk on to the egg mixture, whisking all the time.

2 Strain through a fine chinois or sieve back into the pan and cook over a low heat, stirring with a wooden spoon, until the custard begins to thicken and thinly coat the back of the spoon, about 2–3 minutes. Do not allow to boil as the custard will curdle. Cover the surface with damp greaseproof paper to prevent a skin forming and allow to cool. Then pour into a large shallow bowl, or individual serving bowls, cover with cling film and chill.

3 To make the meringues, whisk the egg whites with a squeeze of lemon juice in a clean, grease-free bowl, using a hand-held electric whisk or balloon whisk, until they form soft peaks. Whisk in the sugar, a spoonful at a time. Once it is all incorporated, continue to whisk for 2 minutes longer.

4 Pour the milk into a large shallow pan and bring to a simmer. Spoon 3 or 4 neat quenelles of meringue into the simmering milk and poach, uncovered, for about 2 minutes. Using a slotted spoon, carefully turn each meringue over and poach for another 2 minutes. Do not cover with a pan lid or the meringues will collapse. When cooked, lift out the meringues with the spoon and float on the coffee custard. Repeat to cook the remaining meringue. Allow to cool.

5 For the caramel, mix the caster sugar, glucose and 2 tablespoons cold water in a heavy-based pan and leave to stand for 10 minutes. Place the pan over a low heat to dissolve the sugar slowly, stirring once or twice. When the liquid is crystal clear, raise the heat and bubble until the syrup turns a rich dark brown caramel (but don't stir, or stop watching). Immediately remove from the heat and carefully drizzle the caramel over the meringues. Leave to stand for 10 minutes before serving, so the caramel sets to a crunchy topping.

6 free-range egg yolks
90g soft light brown sugar
250ml double cream
250ml whole milk
50ml espresso coffee or strong
    instant coffee

Meringue:
2 egg whites
squeeze of lemon juice
100g caster sugar
300ml whole milk

Caramel:
60g caster sugar
1 teaspoon liquid glucose

MERINGUE QUENELLES

Dip a dessertspoon into a bowl of hot water to warm it slightly, then dry. Dip the spoon sideways into the meringue and curl to take up an oval. Immediately, tip the quenelle out sideways into the simmering milk to poach.

my baked alaskas

Instead of baking in a very hot oven which can be unpredictable, I envelop individual alaskas in Italian meringue and wave a blow-torch over the surface to finish. The effect is stunning and they taste divine. A sugar thermometer is useful here, to check the temperature of the sugar syrup for the meringue. **MAKES 6–8**

Genoise sponge base:

50g butter

4 medium free-range eggs

125g caster sugar

125g plain flour, sifted

Filling:

200g raspberries, lightly crushed

6 scoops good quality ice cream
   (preferably homemade, page 158)

Italian meringue:

180g caster sugar

1½ teaspoons liquid glucose

3 large free-range egg whites

squeeze of lemon juice

1 To make the sponge, melt the butter, then cool to room temperature. Preheat the oven to 190°C, Gas 5. Line a shallow baking tray with baking parchment.

2 Whisk the eggs and sugar in a large heatproof bowl over a pan of gently simmering water, using a hand-held electric whisk, until the mixture is pale, thick and creamy. It should leave a trail as you lift the beaters. Remove the bowl from the heat and whisk for a further 3–5 minutes to cool.

3 Using a large metal spoon, gently fold in the flour. Now, drizzle the runny butter down the side of the bowl and fold this in very gently. Carefully pour on to the prepared tray and gently spread to a 1cm thickness, making sure the surface is level. (It doesn't matter if the mixture doesn't extend to the sides of the tray.) Bake for about 10 minutes, until golden and just firm to the touch. Leave on the tray for 10 minutes, then turn out on to a wire rack and peel off the paper.

4 To make the meringue, put the sugar, glucose and 3 tablespoons water into a medium heavy-based saucepan and leave to stand for 10 minutes, then dissolve over a medium heat, stirring once or twice. When the liquid is clear, increase the heat and boil until the syrup registers 120°C on a sugar thermometer.

5 In the meantime, whisk the egg whites with a squeeze of lemon juice in a clean, grease-free bowl, using a hand-held electric whisk or balloon whisk, until they form soft peaks. With the beaters still whirling, slowly pour the hot syrup down the side of the bowl and continue beating on full speed for 10 minutes to a firm, glossy meringue. Set to one side.

6 Using a 6–7cm cutter, cut out 12 discs of the baked sponge. Place six on a tray, lined with cling film and top with a layer of crushed raspberries.

7 Now finish one at a time, so the ice cream doesn't melt. Place a neat scoop of ice cream (the same diameter as the discs) on the raspberries, then top with a plain sponge disc. Quickly cover the top and sides with meringue, swirling it attractively. Repeat to finish the rest of the alaskas, then place, uncovered, in the freezer until ready to serve.

8 To serve, place each alaska on a serving plate and wave a cook's blow-torch lightly and quickly over each meringue to colour. This only takes seconds – take care to avoid over-scorching. Serve at once.

CHEF'S SECRET Using Italian meringue is the secret here. Because it is made with a boiling syrup, it is effectively cooked, so there's no need to finish the Alaskas in the oven. It is also very stable and will hold up well while you assemble them. Italian meringue doesn't freeze solid, so there's no problem serving the puddings from the freezer.

calvados rice brûlées

As a twist on classic crème brûlées, I spoon a rich, creamy rice pudding into ramekins, scatter demerara sugar over the surface and caramelise the topping. The simple combination of flavours works brilliantly. Serve with apple tuiles (see below) or sliced fresh fruit, such as peaches or mango, if you haven't time to make the tuiles. **SERVES 6**

90g pudding rice
250ml whole milk
250ml double cream
90g caster sugar
6 free-range egg yolks
2 tablespoons Calvados
6 tablespoons demerara sugar

To serve:
Apple Tuiles (see below), or peach or
   mango slices

1 To make the pudding, put the rice into a large non-stick saucepan with the milk, cream and caster sugar. Bring slowly to the boil, then turn the heat down and simmer for about 25 minutes, stirring occasionally until the rice is soft and plump and the milk is mostly absorbed.

2 Meanwhile, beat the egg yolks in a bowl until thick and creamy. Slowly mix in the rice pudding, then return to the pan and cook, stirring, over a low heat for a couple of minutes or so until it starts to thicken. Do not overheat or it will curdle.

3 Immediately remove from the heat and stir in the Calvados, then divide the rice pudding between six ramekins and allow to cool. Chill until required.

4 When ready to serve, sprinkle demerara sugar thickly on top of each pudding and wave a blow-torch over the surface to melt and caramelise the sugar. Don't do this in advance or the sugar will dissolve into a syrup rather than caramelise.

5 Serve the puddings as soon as they are all caramelised. Set the ramekins on small plates, with apple tuiles (see below) or sliced peach or mango on the side.

APPLE TUILES Preheat the oven to its lowest setting, maximum 100°C, Gas ¼. Core, but do not peel a Granny Smith apple, then cut into thin, even slices. Cover a large baking sheet with a non-stick silicone liner. Dip the apple slices, one at a time, into Stock Syrup (page 164), then lay on the silicone mat, making sure they are not touching. Place in the oven until dry and crisp, about 2 hours. Remove to a wire rack to cool and crisp.

crème anglaise

A good crème anglaise – or homemade custard sauce – tastes superb, and it can be served either warm or chilled. It complements so many desserts, from sophisticated fruit tarts through to homely puddings and pies, and of course it is an integral part of some recipes, including trifles and classic bavarois. Crème anglaise will keep for 2–3 days in the fridge as long as you cover the surface to stop a skin forming. And although it cannot be frozen as it is, you can churn it in an ice cream machine to make wonderful ice cream. You may be surprised by the suggestion of UHT milk, but it does make the custard more stable. **MAKES ABOUT 600ml**

1 Put the milk and cream into a heavy-based saucepan with 1 tablespoon of the sugar (this will help to stop the mixture boiling over).

2 Using a balloon whisk, beat the rest of the sugar and egg yolks together in a large heatproof bowl. Slit the vanilla pods lengthways, scoop out the tiny seeds with the tip of a knife and add them to the yolk and sugar mix.

3 Add the empty vanilla pods to the milk and cream, then slowly bring to the boil. As the liquid starts to creep up the sides of the pan, gradually pour on to the sugary yolks, beating well.

4 Strain the mixture through a sieve back into the pan, then place over a low heat. Stir constantly with a wooden spoon until the custard thickens slightly – enough to thinly coat the back of the spoon. If you draw a finger along the back of the spoon, it should leave an impression. A sugar thermometer can be used to check when the custard is cooked sufficiently – the temperature should be 82–84°C.

5 Immediately remove the pan from the heat and strain the custard back into the bowl through a fine sieve. Cover and allow to cool, stirring occasionally to prevent a skin forming. Chill until required (or churn into ice cream).

250ml whole milk, preferably UHT
250ml double cream
50g caster sugar
6 large free-range egg yolks
2 vanilla pods

FLAVOURED CRÈME ANGLAISE You can infuse the creamy milk with other flavourings, omitting the vanilla pods. For a minted crème anglaise, for example, add the leaves from 6 mint sprigs to the hot creamy milk and set aside to infuse for 30 minutes, then remove the leaves and return the liquid to the boil before adding to the yolk and sugar mix.

classic vanilla ice cream

We only ever serve homemade ice cream in our restaurants. There is always a good variety of flavoured ice creams in the freezers to complement our desserts, and most of them are based on crème anglaise. Pale yellow and speckled with tiny black vanilla seeds, real vanilla ice cream is far superior to bought ice cream. The secret to success is a smooth texture, and using an ice cream machine is the best way to achieve this. If you haven't got one already, then I recommend you to invest in a good quality domestic ice cream machine with a built-in freezer motor. **MAKES ABOUT 1.2 LITRES**

500ml whole milk, preferably UHT
500ml double cream
100g caster sugar
12 large free-range egg yolks
4 vanilla pods

1 Make the crème anglaise (following the method on page 157). Cool quickly over a bowl of iced water and chill thoroughly.

2 Pour the chilled crème anglaise into an ice cream machine and churn until thick enough to scoop. Either serve straightaway or transfer to a freezerproof plastic tub, seal and put in the freezer. (If you do not have an ice cream machine, freeze the chilled crème anglaise in a shallow container, beating thoroughly at least three times during freezing.)

3 To enjoy the ice cream at its best, eat within a week, allowing it to soften at room temperature for about 10 minutes before scooping. For convenience, you may wish to scoop the soft ice cream into balls and open freeze these on a non-stick tray, ready to serve (or pack into a plastic tub if not serving at once). As ice cream readily absorbs the flavours of food stored alongside it, containers must be well sealed.

VANILLA FANS These attractive decorations are simply made from 'spent' pods. As you scrape the vanilla seeds out (for your crème anglaise, perhaps) make sure you keep one end of the pod intact. Then, using the tip of a very sharp, thin bladed knife, slit each pod lengthways as many times as you can, keeping the end intact. Place on a baking tray lined with greaseproof paper and spread out the strands. Repeat to make as many vanilla fans as you need, then cover with another sheet of greaseproof paper and place another baking tray on top. Bake at 180°C, Gas 4 for 20–25 minutes. When the kitchen fills with the aroma of vanilla you know they are ready. Remove and cool. Use to decorate ice creams and other desserts.

VARIATIONS

By adding different flavours to the crème anglaise before churning it, you can create a variety of flavoured ice creams. These are some of my favourites.

Orange flower water Omit the vanilla. Add 2–3 tablespoons orange flower water to the crème anglaise as it cools.

Cinnamon Substitute the vanilla pods with 2 cinnamon sticks and 1 teaspoon ground cinnamon.

Mint Omit the vanilla. Infuse the hot milk with a large sprig of mint and set aside until cold. Remove the mint, return the milk to the boil and continue as above.

Caramel Before you start making the crème anglaise, gently heat 100g sugar with 1 tablespoon cold water and 40g butter in a heavy-based pan, stirring until dissolved. Increase the heat and cook until the liquid turns golden brown. Immediately remove from the heat and whisk in the milk and cream for the custard. Then proceed with the recipe for crème anglaise.

Rum and raisin Warm 6–8 tablespoonfuls raisins in 100ml each dark rum and Stock Syrup (page 164), then remove from the heat and macerate for 24 hours. Drain and add to the crème anglaise before churning.

white chocolate ice cream

Not all ice creams have a crème anglaise base. This one is simply a mixture of melted white chocolate, cream and milk, combined with an inert sugar, liquid glucose, to keep it smooth. We have very fast freezing machines in our kitchens, which keep the mixture churning until it is smooth and firm enough to scoop into balls. At home, I suggest that after churning the mixture in your domestic ice cream machine, you transfer it to a suitable container and leave it in the freezer for an hour or two before scooping into balls. Good quality white chocolate is essential. **MAKES ABOUT 900ml**

1 Break up the chocolate into a large heatproof bowl and add the remaining ingredients. Place the bowl over a pan of gently simmering water and heat slowly, stirring frequently, until the chocolate melts smoothly into the liquid. Don't allow the mixture to become too hot otherwise the chocolate might 'seize'. It should be just warm enough for the chocolate to melt and blend smoothly.
2 Remove the bowl from the pan and pour the mixture into a cold bowl. Leave until quite cold, then pour into an ice cream machine and churn until it is as thick as possible. Scoop into a freezerproof container and freeze for 2–3 hours or until it is firm enough to scoop into balls.
3 For convenience, you can scoop the ice cream into small balls and open freeze these on a tray lined with a sheet of baking parchment. Freeze until solid, then place in a freezerproof container and keep frozen until ready to serve.

160g white chocolate
250ml double cream
500ml whole milk
50g icing sugar
140g pot liquid glucose

CHEF'S TIP Liquid glucose is available from pharmacists and the baking section of larger supermarkets.

Fruit

Like vegetables, I love to make the most of seasonal fruits and, similarly, I am influenced by favourites from my childhood. I grew up with traditional country fruits – plums, pears and apples plucked from trees, and luscious summer berries gathered at every opportunity.

Semi-wild rhubarb grew in our garden, and I've eaten more rhubarb crumbles than I could possibly remember. If we were hungry before 'tea' was ready, we would be given a stick of raw rhubarb and a pot of sugar – the ultimate dipstick. Those happy memories later inspired me to create a roasted rhubarb and custard crème brûlée, which was a huge success at the Aubergine, my first restaurant. It is the satisfaction of taking an everyday ingredient and getting the maximum from it that drives me to be creative.

Desserts have certainly moved forward from my student days. I remember learning how to massacre fresh pineapple, by pulverising the pulp, mixing it with cassis and lots of whipped cream, then piling it back into the shell. I have no idea why Pineapple Romanof was the highlight of the dessert trolley.

Now I prefer to treat fruit with respect. Plump ripe plums, pink-blushed apricots and fragrant Italian peaches deserve to be appreciated in their natural form. You cannot get much simpler than roasted peaches on brioche toast. But if we want to take this dish a stage further, by steeping the peaches in a fresh basil syrup or scattering them with crystallised coriander leaves, we can do so without masking the flavours

knickerbocker glories

This is my chic version of the favourite British sundae that takes its name from the striped pantaloons worn by Victorian ladies at the seaside. Here tall glasses are filled with delicate layers of fresh orange jelly, panna cotta, crushed amaretti and sliced peaches, then topped with ice cream and a flamboyant fruit finish to serve. **SERVES 4–6**

Orange Jelly:

700ml fresh orange juice

2–3 tablespoons icing sugar

3 sheets leaf gelatine (or 2 teaspoons
    powdered gelatine)

Panna cotta:

4 sheets leaf gelatine (or 3 teaspoons
    powdered gelatine)

600ml double cream

150ml milk

150g caster sugar

grated zest of 1 orange

2 tablespoons white rum (optional)

To serve:

75–100g strawberries, finely chopped

6–8 amaretti biscuits, crushed

2 ripe peaches, thinly sliced

8–10 small scoops of good quality
    vanilla ice cream (preferably
    homemade, page 158)

dried pineapple and star fruit slices
    (optional, see below)

1 For the jelly, put the orange juice into a pan with the icing sugar to taste and boil to reduce to about 500ml. Meanwhile, soak the gelatine leaves in cold water until softened. (Or soak powdered gelatine in 2 tablespoons cold water until spongy.)

2 Remove the gelatine leaves from the cold water and squeeze out excess water, then slide them into the hot orange liquid (or add the softened gelatine) and stir briskly until dissolved. Cool to room temperature. Pour 2 tablespoons into each glass and chill until set. Pour the rest into a shallow bowl and chill until set.

3 For the panna cotta, soak the gelatine leaves in cold water until floppy. (Or soak powdered gelatine in 2 tablespoons cold water until spongy.)

4 Slowly bring the cream and milk to the boil in a large saucepan, stirring. Lower the heat and bubble gently for about 5 minutes to reduce by about a third. Remove the gelatine leaves from the cold water and squeeze out excess water. Take the pan off the heat, stir in the sugar and orange zest, then slide in the gelatine (or add the softened gelatine), stirring until dissolved. Cool slightly, then mix in the rum, if using. Transfer to a bowl and set aside to cool.

5 Pour 2 tablespoons of panna cotta on top of the set jelly in each glass and chill to set. Pour the rest into a shallow bowl and chill until set.

6 Turn the set jelly out of the shallow bowl on to a sheet of baking parchment and chop finely, using a sharp knife dipped in cold water. Add a thin layer of finely chopped strawberries to each glass, then a layer of chopped jelly.

7 Stir the softly set panna cotta in the bowl, then spoon a layer on top of the chopped jelly. Add crushed amaretti, then arrange the peach slices on top. Finally, as a crowning glory, top the peaches with two scoops of vanilla ice cream and finish with dried fruit slices or sliced strawberries. Serve immediately.

DRIED FRUIT SLICES Oven-dried wafer-thin slices of firm fruit, such as pineapple, apple, banana and star fruit (illustrated right), make a stunning decoration. Simply cut slightly under-ripe fruit into very fine slices, using a sharp, serrated fruit knife. Sprinkle fruit that is liable to discoloration, such as banana, with lemon juice. Dip the fruit slices quickly into Stock Syrup (page 164), shake off excess, then lay on baking sheets lined with silicone cooking liners. Leave in the oven on its lowest setting for a good 2 hours until firm and almost translucent. The slices will crisp up on cooling. Store in airtight plastic containers for up to a week.

tropical fruit salad with pomegranate seeds

Make the most of tropical fruits during the winter when they are in good supply and homegrown fruits are limited. Put them together in a vibrant fruit salad to brighten the winter days. Pomegranates are in season from late autumn through to the spring and their fragrant, juicy seeds add a special quality to this salad. Vary the flavour of the stock syrup according to taste. I suggest aromatic Angostura Bitters and a dash of grenadine syrup to accentuate the pomegranate flavour. **SERVES 6–8**

250ml Stock Syrup (see below)

juice of 2 lemons

1 tablespoon Angostura Bitters

2–3 tablespoons grenadine syrup

1 medium ripe pineapple

1 large ripe mango

1 large peach

1 Asian pear (nashi)

1 star fruit

2 kiwi fruit, peeled

225g strawberries, hulled

1–2 pomegranates

1 papaya (paw paw)

1 Mix the syrup with 100ml boiling water, then stir in the lemon juice, Angostura Bitters and grenadine.

2 Prepare the fruits. Peel the pineapple and remove the 'eyes' with the tip of a vegetable peeler or sharp knife. Cut into quarters, remove the core and cut the flesh into bite-sized chunks. Place in a large bowl and pour on the syrup.

3 Cut the mango down either side of the large stone. Peel away the skin and cut the flesh into small cubes. Add to the bowl.

4 Dip the peach briefly into hot water to loosen the skin, then peel. Cut in half, twist to separate and thinly slice the flesh. Peel, quarter and core the Asian pear, then slice thinly. Slice the star fruit and kiwi fruit. Halve or quarter the strawberries. Add all these fruits to the bowl and stir gently to combine. Chill until ready to serve.

5 To prepare the pomegranate(s), halve vertically, then carefully scrape out the fleshy seeds. It is important to remove all of the creamy yellow membrane, which is very bitter.

6 Add the papaya just before serving. Cut in half, scoop out and discard the seeds, then peel the flesh and cut into small chunks. Gently stir these into the fruit salad. Transfer to a serving bowl and scatter over the pomegranate seeds.

STOCK SYRUP

This has so many uses, I suggest you make up a quantity of full strength syrup, using 500ml water and 500g sugar. Dissolve the sugar in the water in a heavy-based pan over a low heat, then bring to the boil and boil for 5 minutes. Cool and bottle or pour into a jar and keep in the fridge (for up to 2 weeks) to use as required. For a light stock syrup you will need to dilute it, adding about half the volume of water. Impart character and colour by adding flavourings, such as pared strips of citrus zest, mint sprigs, bruised lemon grass stalks or a dash of liqueur, such as Malibu, Amaretto or Kahlua.

roasted autumn fruits in bramble syrup

Early autumn is the time to feature flavourful, ripe orchard and hedgerow fruits in desserts. For a simple compote, pan-roast apples and pears until lightly caramelised, then macerate in syrup with poire eau-de-vie or Calvados and some crushed blackberries. Serve chilled, with cream. **SERVES 4–6**

1 Quarter, core and slice the apples and pears, but don't peel them. Heat a large heavy-based non-stick frying pan until you can see a faint haze rising.

2 Toss the sliced fruits in the icing sugar, then immediately tip them into the frying pan and spread out in a single layer. Leave for about 20 seconds until the undersides are beginning to caramelise, then turn each piece to lightly colour the other sides. You only need to caramelise the outside – the fruit should still remain firm. Tip the hot fruits into a bowl.

3 Lightly crush the berries in a bowl, using a fork and pour over the syrup. Add the poire eau-de-vie or Calvados, if using, and toss to mix.

4 Add the berries and syrup to the caramelised apples and pears, stir gently, then set aside to cool and allow the flavours to mingle. Cover and chill until required.

5 To serve, give the fruits a gentle stir, then sprinkle with chopped mint if you like. Serve with cream.

2 large fresh Cox's apples
2 large Conference or Williams pears
4 tablespoons icing sugar, sifted
cupful of blackberries or elderberries, about 150g
250ml Stock Syrup (page 164)
2 tablespoons poire eau-de-vie or Calvados (optional)
1 tablespoon chopped mint (optional)

PAN-ROASTING FRUITS

Tossing autumn fruits, such as apples and pears, in icing sugar, then searing them in a very hot, dry pan gives them a fabulous caramelised flavour and colour. Brief cooking is essential, as the fruit slices should remain intact.

pear sorbet

This simple, refreshing sorbet is an ideal palate cleanser to serve between courses, or as a light dessert to round off a rich meal. I find the flavour of red-skinned pears is especially good for sorbets. My favourite is the bright Forelle, which has an amazing flavour, but red Williams and Comice pears work well too. **SERVES 4–6**

6 Forelle, Williams or Comice pears,
   just ripe but still firm
juice of 1 lemon
1 cinnamon stick
4 star anise
1 vanilla pod
250ml Stock Syrup (page 164)

1 Peel, quarter, and core the pears, then cut into chunks. Place in a large pan with the lemon juice, cinnamon and star anise. Slit the vanilla pod lengthways, scrape out the seeds and add them to the pan with the empty pod.

2 Pour the stock syrup over the pears and bring to the boil. Lower the heat and simmer gently for 10–15 minutes, or until the pears soften. Remove the whole spices and vanilla pod. Leave the pears to cool in the liquid, then drain in a sieve over a bowl to save the stock syrup.

3 Purée the pears in a blender or food processor, gradually adding back the reserved stock syrup. Pour the purée into a bowl, cover and chill thoroughly, then churn in an ice cream machine to a thick, soft frozen texture. Either serve at once or transfer to a freezer container, seal and store in the freezer for up to 2 weeks.

4 If you are serving the sorbet from the freezer, allow it to soften slightly at room temperature for 10 minutes. Scoop into balls and serve in small glass dishes, with crisp dessert biscuits if you like.

VARIATION

For an apple and pear sorbet, replace 3 pears with Granny Smiths apples. The sharpness of the apples complements the mellow sweetness of the pears perfectly.

chilled soup of pan-roasted plums

As a refreshing dessert to impress, serve this sensational ice-cold soup rather than a sorbet. For an intense, rich colour, buy dark-skinned plums at their peak of ripeness. Serve in elegant bowls or wide glasses lined with wafer-thin plum slices. A spiral of creamy bio yogurt adds a sophisticated finishing touch – no one will guess it's simply squeezed from a plastic bottle. (Illustrated overleaf) **SERVES 4**

1 Halve and stone the plums and set aside the 6 best halves to serve. Cut the rest into quarters. Heat a wide, shallow heavy-based pan until you can see a faint haze rising.

2 Toss the plum quarters in the icing sugar, then immediately tip them into the pan and spread out in a single layer, adding the cinnamon, vanilla pods, orange zest and star anise. Cook, without moving, for about 20 seconds until beginning to caramelise underneath, then turn to lightly colour the other sides.

3 Mix the stock syrup with 100ml boiling water and the liquid glucose, then pour into the pan. Bring to the boil, then lower the heat and simmer for 10–15 minutes until the plums are softened.

4 Set aside to cool, then remove the cinnamon, vanilla pods, orange zest and star anise. Tip the plums and syrup into a blender or food processor and whiz to a smooth purée. Rub this through a fine chinois or sieve into a bowl with the back of a ladle. Cover the bowl with cling film and chill the soup until required.

5 When ready to serve, slice the reserved plum halves as thinly as possible and use to line the sides of 4 shallow sundae glasses or glass bowls. Carefully pour in the soup. Stir the yogurt until smooth and runny, then trickle on top of the soup and serve.

500g ripe dark red plums
3 tablespoons icing sugar, sifted
2 cinnamon sticks
2 vanilla pods (empty pods with the seeds scraped out will do)
finely pared strips of zest from 1 orange
2 star anise
200ml Stock Syrup (page 164)
1 tablespoon liquid glucose
200g natural creamy bio yogurt, to serve

CHEF'S TIP The simplest finishes are often the most effective. To create the effect illustrated in the photograph, put the yogurt into a clean (squeezable) plastic bottle, replace the top and squeeze a spiral of thin yogurt on to each portion of soup.

CHEF'S TIP We always use leaf gelatine because it softens and dissolves more easily than powdered gelatine, without 'clumping'. However you do need to ensure the liquid you are adding the leaves to is very hot (just below boiling point) or the setting quality may be adversely affected.

melon and grape jelly

Fruit jellies are wonderfully refreshing and always popular with our guests. We serve them in small shot glasses topped with a float of single cream or yogurt. I like to experiment with new flavours – melon with grape is one of our recent successes. You need a fruit that is soft enough to purée, for a clean, fresh taste. A fragrant melon that is almost over-ripe can be used here. Passing the purée through a jelly bag helps to clarify the juice, but it's not vital. **SERVES 4–6**

1 Halve the melon and scoop out the seeds. Using a tiny melon baller, scoop out about 16 balls and set aside.

2 Scoop the remaining melon flesh from the skin and place in a blender or food processor with the lemon juice. Purée until smooth, then whiz in the stock syrup.

3 For a clear jelly, pour the melon purée through a jelly bag suspended from a hook or a large sieve lined with wet muslin, placed over a bowl. Allow the liquid to drip through (rather than force it) to achieve a clear set. It may take an hour or so for all the juice to drip through. You should have around 500ml. (If a crystal clear set isn't your goal, skip this stage.)

4 Soak the gelatine leaves in cold water to cover until floppy. (Or soak powdered gelatine in 2 tablespoons cold water until spongy.)

5 Heat the melon juice until on the point of boiling. Remove the gelatine leaves from the cold water and squeeze out excess. Take the melon juice off the heat and slide in the gelatine (or add the softened gelatine), stirring until dissolved. Set aside to cool.

6 Meanwhile, peel the grapes if you like (but not if you're short of time). Pour a little melon jelly into the base of 4–6 glasses and add a few melon balls and a few grapes. Chill until set. Add another layer of cool liquid jelly and fruit. Chill again until set. Repeat the layers, chilling each to set, until you reach the top of the glasses. Chill until ready to serve.

1 large, well ripened Galia or
    Charentais melon
1 tablespoon lemon juice
100ml Stock Syrup (page 164)
3 sheets leaf gelatine (or 2 teaspoons
    powdered gelatine)
70g small seedless grapes

CHEF'S TIP Setting the fruits within the jelly in layers ensures they are evenly distributed. If you add them altogether the fruit will settle in a layer on the top of the jelly.

ravioli of pineapple with crushed strawberry cream

Wafer-thin slices of fresh pineapple are macerated overnight in stock syrup infused with lemon grass, then sandwiched together with balls of crushed strawberry cream. Simple, and deliciously refreshing. **SERVES 6**

200g caster sugar

1 lemon grass stalk, or strips of finely
   pared zest from 1 lemon

1 large, just ripe pineapple

400g strawberries

200g thick crème fraîche

a little sifted icing sugar, to taste

1 Put the caster sugar into a pan with 400ml water and dissolve over a low heat, then bring to the boil and boil for 5 minutes. Slit the lemon grass in half lengthways, if using. Pour the syrup into a bowl and add the lemon grass or lemon zest to infuse the syrup as it cools. When cold, remove the flavourings.

2 Peel the pineapple and remove the 'eyes' with the tip of a potato peeler or sharp knife. Lay the pineapple horizontally on a board and cut 12 slices as thinly as you possibly can – a long, serrated knife or electric carving knife is ideal for this. Lay the pineapple slices in the syrup as you cut them, making sure that each is well coated in syrup before you add another.

3 Cover and leave to steep overnight in the fridge, or longer, until they soften. Drain off the syrup and dab each slice with kitchen paper to dry slightly.

4 Crush the strawberries with a fork to a rough purée. Beat the crème fraîche until thick and fold in the crushed fruit, sweetening to taste with a little icing sugar. Shape the mixture into six balls, using an ice cream scoop. Choose six of the smallest pineapple slices for the base and place one on each dessert plate. Put a strawberry cream ball in the centre, then position a larger pineapple slice on top. It should drape over the cream – press the sides down slightly to flute them if necessary. That's it – serve as soon as possible.

CHEF'S SECRET Steeping fresh fruit in stock syrup with aromatics lends a subtle flavour and alters the texture of the fruit to give it a different character. In this recipe lemon grass provides the flavour, but other ingredients can be used, such as star anise, vanilla, kirsch or brandy.

caramel bananas en papillote with chocolate sauce

If you enjoy baked bananas as a dessert then this creamy caramel version should please. Bananas are baked in paper pouches along with a rich caramel sauce. Serve the bananas in their pouches for your guests to open at the table, handing round the chocolate sauce in a jug. A scoop of pistachio or roasted almond ice cream would be a perfect finishing touch.
SERVES 4

6 just ripe bananas (not too soft)

Caramel sauce:
300ml double cream
170g light muscovado sugar
4 tablespoons liquid glucose
70g unsalted butter

Chocolate sauce:
80g dark chocolate, at least 60% cocoa solids
120ml double cream
1–2 tablespoons rum (optional)

1 Preheat the oven to 180°C, Gas 4. To make the caramel sauce, pour half the cream into a medium saucepan and add the sugar, glucose and butter. Bring slowly to the boil, stirring until smooth, then simmer for 2 minutes. Remove from the heat and whisk in the remaining cream.

2 Meanwhile, make the chocolate sauce. Break up the chocolate and place in a heatproof bowl with the cream, and rum if using, over a pan of gently simmering water. Leave until melted, stirring once or twice. Remove and stir until smooth, then pour into a jug and set aside to cool.

3 For the papillotes, tear off four sheets of greaseproof paper, measuring 30cm square. Peel the bananas and slit each in half lengthways. Place 3 banana halves in the centre of each paper square and drizzle over the caramel sauce. Fold one half of the paper over the bananas to enclose them and pleat the edges together to seal.

4 Place the papillotes on a baking sheet and bake for 8–10 minutes depending on the ripeness of the bananas. To check that they are softened, press the bananas lightly through the papillotes with the back of a fork.

5 Transfer the papillotes to large serving plates, using a fish slice. They will keep warm for at least 10 minutes. Warn guests to be careful of trapped steam as they open up their parcels. Hand round the chocolate sauce to pour over the bananas.

EN PAPILLOTE This is simply the French term for baking in paper. The food is sealed in the paper parcel, which puffs up and browns in the heat of the oven, while the food inside cooks in the trapped steam. It is an attractive way to present this dish, though you can simply bake the banana halves in a foil-covered shallow dish with the caramel sauce poured over if you prefer.

pain perdu with roasted peaches

Fresh, fragrant peaches are quickly pan-roasted, then piled on top of warm French toasted brioche for a fast dessert, which can also be served as a brunch. For a limited season, August to September, we get supplies of superb Italian white peaches – for me one of the great treats of the summer. You can, of course, use sweet yellow peaches here, or even nectarines. Top with a dollop of mascarpone or whipped cream and eat the pain perdu with a knife and fork. **SERVES 4**

1 Immerse the peaches in a bowl of boiling hot water for barely 30 seconds, then remove with a slotted spoon and peel away the skins as soon as the fruit is cool enough to handle. Score each peach vertically around the middle to the stone, and twist the halves to separate. Cut the halves into quarters or eighths depending on size.

2 Heat half the butter in a heavy-based frying pan and toss in the peaches. Sprinkle with icing sugar and continue to cook over a high heat until nicely caramelised, about 2–3 minutes. Remove the fruits to a plate and keep warm. Wipe out the pan.

3 Pour the beaten eggs into a shallow dish (large enough to take a slice of brioche). Heat half of the remaining butter with 1 tablespoon of oil in the pan until the butter stops foaming.

4 Quickly dip a brioche slice in the egg, turn to coat the other side, then lift out and add to the pan. Cook over a medium-high heat for 45 seconds or until golden brown, then flip over and cook the other side for about 30 seconds until nicely golden brown. Remove to a warm plate and keep warm. Repeat with the remaining brioche slices, adding more butter and oil to the pan as necessary.

5 As soon as they are all cooked, place the brioche slices on warm serving plates and spoon the peaches on top. Add a scoop of mascarpone or whipped cream, dust with icing sugar and serve.

4 large peaches, or 8 smaller ones
100g butter
3–4 tablespoons icing sugar, plus
  extra to dust
2 large free-range eggs, beaten
1–2 tablespoons sunflower oil
4 slices brioche loaf
mascarpone or whipped double
  cream, to serve

PAIN PERDU 'Lost bread' as it is literally translated, has been a favourite way of using up slightly stale bread for centuries. Made with fresh brioche it is a great base for other pan-roasted fruits, such as plums and caramelised apples, compotes of apricots and pears, and fresh berries, such as blueberries trickled with maple syrup.

summer berry kebabs with lavender honey dip

Berries and cream are the ultimate summer sensation. Here flavourful berries are skewered on to dried lavender stalks and served with a lavender infused cream, for an easy dessert that's perfect for al fresco eating. The luscious, fragrant cream serves as a dip. For more robust skewers, use long thin wooden satay sticks instead of the dried lavender stalks. Use any combination of summer fruits – adding cubes of peach, mango or pineapple, if you like. **SERVES 4**

2 tablespoons caster sugar

4 dried lavender heads

150g mascarpone

150ml whipping cream

2 teaspoons clear honey

250g small strawberries or wild
  strawberries (fraises de bois)

125g raspberries or loganberries

125g blueberries

125g blackberries

50g redcurrants

50g white currants

To serve:
about 12 long dried stalks of lavender
  or thin wooden satay sticks

1 Dissolve the caster sugar in 4 tablespoons of water in a small pan over a low heat until clear, then add the lavender heads and simmer for 2 minutes. Allow to cool, then strain the syrup and reserve.

2 Beat the mascarpone and cream together until softly stiff, then fold in the sugar syrup and honey. Pour into a small bowl and chill.

3 Hull the strawberries. Skewer together with the other fruits on dried lavender stalks or thin satay sticks. Chill until required.

4 Place the bowl of cream on a serving plate and arrange the fruit kebabs around. Sprinkle the cream with a few lavender flowers if liked.

LAVENDER INFUSIONS
I use lavender flowers to infuse sugar syrups, creamy custards, even chocolate ganache – the light floral fragrance subtly enhances sweet flavours to delicious effect. To concentrate the flavour, we use dried rather than fresh flowers. Florists specialising in dried flowers are a good source of supply. Alternatively pick your own lavender and hang the stems in a warm, dry kitchen, or airing cupboard to dry.

Flour: breads, pastries and cakes

I consider myself a pretty good baker. I love it. Everyone should learn how to bake bread, and do some elementary cake making, if only to appreciate the amazing smells that waft from the oven. My Mum, Helen, made wonderful cakes. She didn't take a technical approach, she didn't understand the chemistry – to make great cakes you don't need to. Her carrot cake, scones and lemon cakes were deliciously uncomplicated and I devoured them in no time. Eating and football were my two great passions. Mum's approach was wholesome and simple, as all good baking should be.

Bread making, however, does require a basic understanding of how the simple components – flour, yeast and water – work together. For several months during my early training, I had the responsibility for the night baking at Le Gavroche, and later followed this up with a similar stint in Guy Savoy's Paris kitchen. I'll never forget the night the bread oven broke down at 3am. In panic, I rang the head chef at his home to ask for help ... his reply was unrepeatable. The bread oven was repaired first thing in the morning and I had to work like crazy to ensure rolls and bread were ready for the lunch service. The most important lesson for me from those early days was that making bread is like making love – it's a passion not an item. So no bread machines for me. It's a hands-on job. I like to feel the live dough rising, almost pulsating as I knead and shape, watch and smell. No two loaves ever come out the same. They each have a personality.

pain de mie

This gorgeous French bread is a cross between a brioche and a simple white loaf. It is quite to easy to make, especially if you have a mixer with a dough hook. The secret is to make a yeast 'sponge' first to get the yeast active. The dough can be baked free form as a cob, or in a round tin, or shaped into 8 rolls. Fresh yeast will give the best texture and flavour, though you can use dried yeast. Pain de Mie is best eaten within a day or two. **MAKES 1 LARGE LOAF**

15g fresh yeast

125ml whole milk, warmed until tepid (20°C)

125g plain white flour (preferably organic, unbleached)

160g strong white flour (preferably organic, unbleached)

1 teaspoon crushed Maldon salt, or fine sea salt

20g butter, in pieces

2 teaspoons caster sugar

4 tablespoons cold milk

semolina, to sprinkle

oil, to brush

1 Crumble the yeast into a medium bowl and whisk in the milk until dissolved. Then beat in the 125g plain flour until quite smooth. Cover with cling film and leave in a warm place (such as an airing cupboard at about 28°C) for about 1 hour to 'sponge'.

2 Meanwhile, sift the strong flour and salt into a bowl and rub in the butter, then stir in the sugar. Make a well in the centre.

3 When the 'sponged' dough is ready, add to the flour well with the cold milk and mix to a soft dough. Knead vigorously for 5–10 minutes, either in a machine with a dough hook, or by hand on a very lightly floured work surface. The dough is ready when you can press it and leave a thumbprint.

4 Place the dough in a bowl, cover with cling film and leave in a warm spot (28°C) for about 1 hour until doubled in bulk.

5 Knock back the dough on a clean surface and shape into a large oval. Sprinkle the top with semolina, pressing lightly so it stays in place. Oil a heavy baking sheet and sprinkle the base liberally with semolina. Place the dough on the baking sheet and leave to prove until doubled in size, about 45–60 minutes. Meanwhile, preheat the oven to 200°C, Gas 6.

6 Spray the baking sheet around the risen dough with cold water, then immediately bake for 10 minutes. Reduce the setting to 180°C, Gas 4 and bake for a further 15–20 minutes or until golden brown and crisp, and the loaf sounds hollow when tapped on the base. Remove and slide on to a wire rack to cool.

PAIN DE MIE ROLLS Shape the dough into 8 balls, roll the tops back and forth a few times to smooth, then press them into a bowl containing some semolina. Place on a baking sheet lined with baking parchment and cover loosely with cling film. Leave to prove until doubled in size, then bake at 200°C, Gas 6 for just 12 minutes.

USING DRIED YEAST If you cannot obtain fresh yeast, I recommend ordinary dried active yeast here (rather than fast-action). Blend 1½ teaspoons with a little of the tepid milk and 2 tablespoons of the soft flour. Wait for a few minutes until the mixture begins to bubble, then mix in the remaining tepid milk and soft flour. Continue as above.

sun-dried tomato fougasse

Fougasse is the great Provençal rich flat bread, originally an orange-scented sweet dough, but now more often made with a savoury twist. This version, flavoured with sun-dried tomatoes and herbs, is my favourite – especially eaten al fresco on a warm summer evening. To give the dough a head start, you need to make a yeast 'sponge'. (Illustrated overleaf) **MAKES 2**

1 To make the 'sponge', place 140g of the flour in a large bowl and mix in 1½ teaspoons of the yeast. Heat 120ml of the water until tepid (20°C), add to the flour and beat for 1–2 minutes until smooth. Cover with cling film and leave in a warm place (such as an airing cupboard) for about 1½ hours to 'sponge'.

2 Now heat the remaining 180ml water until tepid and beat into the 'sponged' mixture with the rest of the strong flour, the rye flour, salt, remaining yeast and 1 tablespoon of the olive oil. Mix thoroughly.

3 Turn the dough on to a lightly floured surface and knead firmly for about 5 minutes, until you have a smooth, fairly soft dough. Transfer to a clean bowl, cover with cling film and leave to rise in a warm place (at about 28°C) for 30 minutes or so, until it begins to rise.

4 Meanwhile, pat the sun-dried tomatoes dry with kitchen paper if necessary and cut into small bite-sized pieces. Knock the risen dough back on a lightly floured surface. Using a rolling pin, roll out to a 40cm square. Scatter the tomato pieces and chives or oregano over the dough.

5 Fold the sides into the middle, then fold the bottom third up to the centre and the top third over that – to give a rectangle, about 20 x 13cm. Roll (or pull and pat) the dough out again to a square, fold and roll one more time.

6 Divide the dough in half and shape each piece into a log. Keep one covered while you roll out the other to an oval, about 25–30cm long and 10–12cm wide.

7 Lift the dough on to a baking sheet lined with baking parchment and slash the top quite deeply at an angle, either side of the middle, using a very sharp knife. Repeat to make another fougasse with the remaining dough.

8 Brush with a little more olive oil and cover loosely with cling film. Leave in a warm place until doubled in size, about 30 minutes.

9 Meanwhile, preheat the oven to 220°C, Gas 7. Spray the baking sheets around each fougasse with water, then immediately bake for about 15 minutes until browned and crisp, swapping the baking sheets halfway through cooking. Brush the fougasse liberally with the remaining olive oil as they cool.

VARIATION Scatter 100g chopped pitted black or green olives and 1 tablespoon snipped rosemary over the rolled-out dough, instead of sun-dried tomatoes and chives. Sprinkle the top with crushed Maldon sea salt flakes just before baking.

420g strong white flour (preferably organic, unbleached), plus extra to dust

7g sachet fast-action dried yeast

300ml bottled still spring water

80g rye flour

1½ teaspoons crushed Maldon salt or fine sea salt

6 tablespoons extra virgin olive oil

Filling:

125g semi-soft sun-dried tomatoes or a 280g jar, drained

4 tablespoons chopped chives, or 1–2 teaspoons dried oregano

sourdough

For this classic sourdough, you need to make a yeast starter, a good 4–5 days ahead. Organic apple juice, yogurt and currants introduce natural yeasts that feed on the flours and bubble into lively, tasty ferments. A warm dry place, like an airing cupboard or draught-free spot in a warm kitchen, helps the fermentation process. **MAKES 2 OR 3 LOAVES**

Starter:

125g strong flour (preferably organic, unbleached)

125g rye flour, plus up to 150g extra to sprinkle

170ml organic (unfiltered) apple juice

150g organic low-fat live bio yogurt

50g organic currants, washed and dried

Bread:

10g fresh yeast, or 2 teaspoons dried active yeast and a little caster sugar

200ml tepid spring water (20°C)

300g rye starter (from above)

375g strong white flour (preferably organic, unbleached)

125g strong wholemeal flour

50g rye flour

2 teaspoons Maldon salt, finely crushed or fine sea salt

100ml organic (unfiltered) apple juice

extra white flour and semolina, to dust

sunflower oil, to oil

1 For the starter, place both flours in a plastic bowl with the apple juice, yogurt and currants. Beat well for about 5 minutes to a smooth, thick batter, then sprinkle the top lightly with rye flour. Cover and leave in a warm place (such as an airing cupboard at about 28°C) for 24 hours.

2 Lightly beat the starter and sprinkle again with rye flour. Cover and store as above. Repeat this process for a total of 5 days by which time you should have a lively fermenting starter, about 600g. You need to use half. (Put the other half in a clean plastic container and refrigerate or freeze for another batch of sourdough.)

3 For the bread, crumble the fresh yeast, if using, into a bowl, add the tepid water and stir briskly to dissolve. If using dried yeast, mix with the water and 2 pinches of caster sugar and leave for about 10 minutes until it begins to 'sponge.'

4 Mix the yeast liquid with the rye starter and half the white flour. Cover loosely with cling film and leave in a warm place until the mixtures bubbles, about 1 hour.

5 Combine the wholemeal, rye and remaining white flour with the salt in a warm large mixing bowl. Add the bubbling yeast dough and apple juice. Mix with your hands until the dough no longer feels sticky, then turn out on to a clean surface.

6 Knead well, only dusting the surface very lightly with flour if necessary – as you knead, the dough will become smooth and less sticky. The dough is ready when you can press it and leave a thumbprint. Place in a lightly oiled bowl, cover with cling film and leave in a warm place for about 1 hour until doubled in size.

7 Knock back the dough, knead again for about 3 minutes, then return to the bowl, cover and leave to prove for another hour.

8 Knock the dough back again and divide into 2 or 3 equal pieces. Roll these into batons, 25–30cm long. Oil a large non-stick heavy baking sheet and dust with semolina. Place the batons well apart on this and make 4 or 5 diagonal slashes along each one with a razor-sharp knife. Sprinkle lightly with white flour and leave in a warm spot until risen by about a third. Meanwhile, preheat the oven to 250°C, Gas 9 and boil the kettle.

9 Put a roasting tin, half-filled with boiling water on a lower oven shelf. Place the baking sheet holding the batons on a higher shelf and bake for 5 minutes. Then turn the temperature down to 200°C, Gas 6 and cook for another 25–30 minutes until the crust is mid-brown in colour and the bread sounds hollow when tapped underneath. Cool on a wire rack.

APPLE AND SAGE SOURDOUGH This is delicious served with cheese. Make up the basic sourdough to the end of stage 6. Roll out to a large rectangle, about 1cm thick, and scatter evenly almost to the edges with a medium Bramley apple, peeled, cored and cut into 1.5cm chunks. Fold the sides into the middle, then pull the top down a third and the bottom up and over that, to make a rectangle. Roll and fold once more, then cover and leave to rise again for about 1 hour. Continue from stage 8.

buckwheat blinis

Large wafer-thin crêpes made with buckwheat flour are popular across northern France. For smaller, thicker blinis, the buckwheat batter is fermented with a little yeast to lighten and flavour it, then cooked in small cast-iron blini pans. If you haven't any of these pans, then cook spoonfuls of batter in a large heavy-based frying pan, like drop scones. The blinis won't be as neatly rounded, but the flavour and texture will be just as good. Soured cream and caviar is the traditional topping, but blinis make good starters with less expensive toppings (see below). Allow two per person. **SERVES 6 AS A STARTER**

1 Put the tepid milk into a jug, crumble in the fresh yeast and stir briskly until dissolved.

2 Mix the two flours and salt together in a large bowl, standing on a damp cloth to hold it steady. Make a well in the centre and add the egg yolk and half of the yeast mixture. Beat to a thick batter with a whisk, gradually adding the rest of the yeasty milk and the beer.

3 Cover with cling film and leave in a warm spot for about an hour or until bubbles start to appear and the mixture looks as if it is expanding. Alternatively, for a slow rise, leave the batter in the fridge; it will take about 4 hours to bubble.

4 Whisk the egg whites in a clean bowl to soft peaks, then whisk in the sugar. Beat a spoonful of the whisked egg whites into the blini batter to loosen it, then fold in the remaining whites, using a spatula.

5 Take one or two cast-iron blini pans, about 8cm in diameter. Melt a knob of butter in each pan and heat until you can feel a strong heat rising. Spoon a ladleful of batter into each pan and cook for 1–1½ minutes until the surface is covered with tiny bubbles and no longer looks wet on the surface, and the sides look cooked. Loosen the edges with a palette knife, check that the underside is brown, then flip over and cook for a minute on the other side.

6 Stack the blinis in a folded clean tea towel to keep them warm while you cook the rest; you should have sufficient batter to make 12 blinis. Serve warm, with your preferred toppings (see below).

100ml milk, heated until tepid

15g fresh yeast (or fast-action dried yeast, see below)

55g strong plain flour

45g buckwheat flour

½ teaspoon fine sea salt

1 free-range egg yolk

2 tablespoons beer

2 free-range egg whites

2 teaspoons sugar

butter, to fry

USING DRIED YEAST

If fresh yeast isn't available, use 2 teaspoons fast-action dried yeast. Simply mix the granules straight into the two flours with the salt, then beat in the tepid milk with the egg yolk and beer as described in step 2.

TOPPINGS Serve blinis warm, topped with a dollop of thick soured cream or crème fraîche and smoked salmon scrunched into rosettes, or folded Parma ham. Or top with lemon mayonnaise and flaked grilled salmon. For an unusual topping, spoon on a little fig jam and top with slices of Duck 'Bresaola' (page 60). The shallot and cep topping (from Caramelised Cep Tarts, page 188) is an ideal vegetarian option.

caramelised cep tarts

Wafer-thin puff pastry discs are covered with a layer of creamy onion purée, then topped with caramelised ceps and Parmesan shavings. This recipe is suitable for vegetarians if you omit the bacon and use white wine rather than chicken stock.

SERVES 4 AS A STARTER OR LIGHT MEAL

350g Puff Pastry (page 190)

50g butter

2 tablespoons olive oil

1 large Spanish onion, thinly sliced

25g smoked bacon or pancetta
   trimmings (optional)

3 tablespoons chicken stock or
   white wine

2 tablespoons double cream

250g fresh ceps, cleaned and thinly
   sliced

2 shallots, finely chopped

1 thyme sprig

sea salt and freshly ground black
   pepper

25g Parmesan cheese, pared into
   shavings, to serve

1 Roll out the pastry to the thickness of a £1 coin and cut out four 12cm discs, using a small saucer as a guide. Prick the dough and place on a heavy non-stick baking sheet. Rest in the refrigerator while you heat the oven to 200°C, Gas 6.

2 Meanwhile, make the onion purée. Heat half the butter and 1 tablespoon olive oil in a saucepan. Add the onion, with the bacon trimmings if using, and sauté gently for up to 15 minutes until softened but not coloured, stirring often. Remove the bacon pieces. Stir in the stock or wine and cream. Season and cook for another few minutes until reduced right down. Transfer to a blender or food processor and whiz until smooth and creamy. Set aside.

3 Cover the pastry discs with baking parchment and place another flat heavy baking sheet on top. Bake for 12 minutes, then remove the top baking sheet and parchment. Return the pastry discs to the oven for up to 3 minutes until golden brown and crisp. Remove and carefully transfer to a wire rack.

4 Heat the remaining butter and olive oil in a sauté pan, then add the sliced ceps and sauté until nicely caramelised, about 5 minutes. Add the shallots, with the leaves from the thyme sprig, and seasoning. Cook for a further 2–3 minutes, then remove from the heat.

5 Lightly warm the onion purée and pastry discs. Spread the onion purée thickly over the pastry and arrange the caramelised ceps on top. Scatter over the Parmesan shavings and serve warm.

VARIATION

When fresh ceps are not in season, or simply for a cheaper option, use thinly sliced, large portobello mushrooms and enhance the flavour with a 10g pack of dried porcini mushrooms. Soak the dried mushrooms in hot water for 10 minutes, then drain, chop and fry with the fresh mushrooms. The soaking liquor can be strained and used instead of the stock or wine.

CHEF'S SECRET I love the light crispness of puff pastry but not all those deep puffy layers. To obtain wafer-thin flat pastry bases, I bake puff pastry discs between two heavy baking sheets. This impedes rising and produces melt-in-the-mouth crisp pastry – the perfect foil for a caramelised shallot and cep topping.

puff pastry

Homemade puff pastry certainly has a richer flavour than ready-made puff, and a wonderful melt-in-the-mouth texture. If a recipe calls for 250g puff pastry use a quarter of this recipe; for 350g use a third, for 500g use half. Make up a batch and divide into portions, freezing any you don't need to use now. **MAKES 1.2kg**

500g butter, cut into chunks

500g plain flour

½ teaspoon fine sea salt

1 teaspoon white wine vinegar

about 300ml ice-cold water

1 Divide the butter into 450g and 50g portions. Set aside 50g of the flour. Sift the rest of the flour with the salt into a bowl and rub in the 50g of the butter until the mixture looks like fine breadcrumbs. This can be done in a food processor.

2 Add the vinegar and trickle in the ice-cold water, mixing with a table knife until it comes together as a smooth dough. You may not need all the water, or you may need a little more. This depends on the flour.

3 Now, mix the remaining 50g flour into the remaining 450g of butter. This is best done using an electric mixer. Spoon this mixture out on to a large sheet of cling film and shape into a rectangle, 14 x 20cm. Wrap well in cling film and chill until firm. Wrap and chill the dough at the same time – both for around 20 minutes.

4 On a lightly floured surface, roll out the dough to a 25 x 35cm rectangle – twice the size of the butter. Make sure the edges and corners are straight and neat. This is one of the secrets of success. If necessary, tease the dough into shape.

5 Place the chilled butter rectangle on the long end of the rolled dough and fold the dough in two to completely enclose the butter. Press the edges of the dough together to seal in the butter.

6 Roll out the dough in one direction only until it is three times the length, making sure none of the butter breaks through.

7 Fold the dough in three, bringing the top third down to the centre, then folding the bottom third on top. Give the dough a quarter turn and roll it out again in one direction, lightly dusting with flour as necessary. Fold as before, keeping those edges neat, then wrap in cling film and chill for another 20 minutes, or longer in warm weather.

8 Unwrap with the fold to the same side as before and roll out for a third time. Fold as before, that is top to centre, then bottom over. Finally, divide into portions as dictated by your recipe.

CHEF'S SECRET Puff pastry rises best when the fat has been incorporated into the flour dough in very fine, even layers. For this reason it is important to always make sure the edges of the dough are as straight as possible when rolling and folding. Simply pat or pull the dough into line. To keep tabs on the number of rollings after each folding, press a fingertip into the corner of the dough to correspond with the number of rollings.

pâte sucrée

This is one of the standard pastries we use for tarts. Make up a big batch and divide into 3 or 4 portions. Wrap portions you don't need to use immediately in freezer film and freeze. For best results, make this pastry in an electric mixer, then knead lightly by hand. **MAKES ABOUT 1kg**

1 Using an electric mixer, beat the butter and sugar together until smooth and creamy, but not fluffy. Split open the vanilla pods, scrape out the seeds and add these to the mixture.

2 With the machine running on slow speed, gradually add the eggs. Stop the machine once or twice and scrape down the sides.

3 Sift the flour and salt together. With the machine on its lowest speed, add the flour in 3 or 4 stages. As soon as the mixture comes together as a crumbly dough, stop the machine.

4 Gather the dough and place on a lightly floured surface. Briefly knead it with your hands until smooth; don't over-work it. Divide into 3 or 4 batches and wrap in cling film. Leave to rest in the refrigerator for 30 minutes before rolling out, freezing any portions you don't need now for later use.

5 Before rolling out, knead the pastry again very lightly. This helps to prevent it cracking as you roll it.

250g butter, softened to room temperature
180g caster sugar
3–4 vanilla pods
2 large free-range eggs, beaten
500g plain flour
½ teaspoon fine sea salt

COOK'S TIP If you divide the pâte sucrée dough into 3 equal portions, each of these portions will be sufficient to line a 21–23 cm tart tin. Double wrap in freezer film to freeze and give the dough a light kneading after thawing.

hazelnut sablés

Thin, light crisp biscuits like these have many applications in our desserts. We sit crème brûlées on them and use them to accompany ice creams, roasted fruits and fruit compotes. They will keep crisp for up to a week in an airtight tin, or you can freeze them and remove a few at a time as you need them. That is, of course, if you can resist nibbling your way through the entire batch, as they are seriously more-ish. **MAKES 20–24**

100g unsalted butter, softened

45g icing sugar, sifted

½ teaspoon fine sea salt

25g toasted chopped hazelnuts

125g plain flour

1 In a bowl, beat together the butter, icing sugar and salt until light and fluffy. Stir in the nuts and flour and mix to a smooth soft dough, kneading gently with your hands. Wrap in cling film and chill for about 30 minutes. Meanwhile, preheat the oven to 180°C, Gas 4.

2 Tear off two sheets of baking parchment, each the size of a heavy baking sheet. Place the dough between the parchment sheets and roll out to a 1cm thickness. Holding the edges of the paper, lift on to the baking sheet and place a second heavy baking sheet on top, so that the dough is sandwiched between both parchment and baking sheets.

3 Bake for 5 minutes, then remove to a heatproof surface and lift off the top baking sheet. With the top baking parchment still in place, roll the half-baked dough as thinly as you can, then remove the parchment. Return to the oven and bake for another 5 minutes or until pale golden.

4 Remove from the oven and, using a 5–6cm cutter, immediately cut out as many rounds as you can while the dough is still soft. Using a palette knife, lift these on to a wire tray to cool and crisp. If the dough starts to harden before you finish cutting, return to the oven for a minute or so to soften. When cool, store the biscuits in an airtight tin.

CHEF'S SECRET Rolling the half baked dough for a second time between layers of parchment halfway through baking, and cutting out the dough after (rather than before) baking is the secret to these ultra-crisp biscuits.

banana and rum tatins

This is one of the recipes that earned my Head Chef at Claridges, Mark Sargeant (or Sarge as he is better known), the Chef of the Year 2002 award. Serve with cream, crème fraîche, or vanilla or rum and raisin ice cream. (Illustrated overleaf) **SERVES 4**

1 Have ready a large cast-iron frying pan (suitable for use in the oven) or a Swiss roll tin. Put the sugar into a heavy-based saucepan and heat very gently until it melts. (You may find it easier if you first saturate the sugar with 2 tablespoons cold water.)

2 Add the butter and melt over a medium heat, shaking the pan to blend the butter with the sugar. Boil to a medium dark brown caramel, but do not allow it to burn. Immediately take off the heat and stir in the rum – it will splutter.

3 Pour the caramel into the cast-iron pan or Swiss roll tin and spread with the back of a spoon to level and cover an area that will take the 4 banana halves; it doesn't need to reach the sides. Cool until set.

4 If using fresh 'virgin' pastry, roll out on a lightly floured surface to the thickness of a £1 coin, then scrunch into a ball and knead lightly until smooth. Roll out again, this time more thinly than before, or roll out trimmings in the same way.

5 Peel each banana, slice in half lengthways, and place rounded-side down on the pastry. Cut the pastry around the bananas, leaving a 1cm border all round, to make half-moon shapes. Transfer the bananas to a board, cut-side down, and drape the pastry crescents over them. Press the pastry to the sides of the bananas and trim away any excess, then place cut-side down on the set caramel. Rest in the fridge for at least 30 minutes. Preheat the oven to 200ºC, Gas 6.

6 When ready to serve, place the tin on a heavy baking sheet and cook in the oven for about 12–15 minutes until the pastry is light golden brown and crisp. Leave to stand for a minute or so, then slide a palette knife under each banana and carefully lift and flip over on to a warmed plate. Trickle over the caramelised pan juices and top with a vanilla fan. Serve with a scoop of ice cream placed on a dried banana slice for optimum effect, or accompany with cream or crème fraîche. Dust lightly with icing sugar to serve.

80g caster sugar
80g butter, in small pieces
2 tablespoons dark rum
300g Puff Pastry (page 190) or
   trimmings (see below)
2 large, slightly unripe bananas

To serve:
Vanilla Fans (page 158)
ice cream, cream or crème fraîche
Dried Banana Slices (page 162,
   optional)
icing sugar, to dust (optional)

CHEF'S SECRET We use a lot of puff pastry and have plenty of trimmings from the first rolling, or 'seconds' as we call them. These trimmings are not discarded, but designated for a different role. We gather them together, mould them gently into rectangles, then wrap and chill to rest. These 'seconds' cook to light, crisp pastry that doesn't rise too much – perfect for the above tatins and our flat tart bases.

CHEF'S SECRET The ingredients for this dessert are simple – the secret lies in the technique. You will need puff pastry that crisps but doesn't rise too much, and the tatins need to be baked just before serving.

croustade of apple and coconut

Before my formative period in the Paris kitchens of the great and good top chefs, I had a wonderful time in the kitchens of the Hotel Diva, located in a ski resort above Nice. When it snowed hard, we were cut off from our suppliers and learnt to be resourceful with dry stores. This comforting, easy dessert was created in those days. Serve it with Crème Anglaise (page 157), ideally infused with a few mint leaves. **SERVES 6**

350g Pâte Sucrée (page 191)
100g sultanas
6 Granny Smiths apples
100g butter
50g demerara sugar
finely grated zest of 1 orange
finely grated zest of 1 lemon
3 tablespoons desiccated coconut,
  lightly toasted
about 100g filo pastry sheets
icing sugar, to dust

1 Roll out the pastry thinly on a lightly floured surface and use to line a 21cm flan tin, that is at least 2.5cm deep. Press the pastry well into the sides and leave about 1cm overhanging the top edge. Prick the base, line with greaseproof paper or foil and baking beans, then rest in the fridge for 30 minutes.

2 Meanwhile, preheat the oven to 200°C, Gas 6. Put the sultanas in a bowl, cover with boiling water and leave for 15 minutes. Drain and pat dry with kitchen paper.

3 Peel, quarter and core the apples, then cut into 1.5cm cubes. Heat half the butter in a large frying pan, toss in the apples and sprinkle the sugar over them. Cook, stirring occasionally, until the apples are just tender and lightly caramelised, about 12 minutes. Remove from the heat and stir in the grated citrus zests, coconut and sultanas. Set aside.

4 Place the flan tin on a baking sheet and bake 'blind' for about 15 minutes. Remove the paper or foil and beans and return the flan case to the oven for 5 minutes to cook the base. With a sharp knife, trim the overhanging pastry until neatly level with the top of the tin.

5 Spoon the apples into the flan case. Melt the remaining butter and use to brush each filo sheet lightly on both sides, scrunching each one like a crumpled tissue. Place on top of the apples to cover them, then dust with icing sugar.

6 Bake the flan for another 12–15 minutes until the filo topping is crisp and golden brown. Dust with a little more icing sugar to serve.

VARIATION
For a different topping, omit the filo. Beat together 120g caster sugar, 120g desiccated coconut and 2 eggs. Spoon this on top of the apples and bake for 12–15 minutes until the topping puffs up slightly and turns golden brown.

CHEF'S SECRET Choosing the right apple for the particular dish will make all the difference to the end result. For apple tarts where the flesh needs to retain a bite, I prefer Granny Smiths or Braeburn apples. For crumbles and apple sauce, Bramleys are a better choice because their flesh cooks to a full-flavoured fluffy pulp. Golden Delicious and those apples with perfect day-glo pink skins don't cook well.

plum and almond tart

This family size version of the little plum tarts we feature on our dessert menus is ideal for a Sunday lunch. It is best served freshly baked and warm. As a variation, you could use mi-cuit prunes instead of plums. **SERVES 6–8**

1 Roll out the pastry on a lightly floured surface to the thickness of a £1 coin and use to line a 25cm flan tin, that is at least 2.5cm deep with a removable base. Press the pastry well into the sides and leave about 1cm overhanging the top edge. Prick the base, line with greaseproof paper or foil and baking beans, then rest in the fridge for 20 minutes.

2 Preheat the oven to 200°C, Gas 6. Place the tart tin on a heavy baking sheet and bake blind for 15 minutes. Remove the paper or foil and beans and return the flan case to the oven for 5 minutes to cook the base. Using a sharp knife, trim the overhanging pastry until neatly level with the top of the tin. Set aside to cool while you make the filling, and lower the oven setting to 150°C, Gas 2.

3 For the filling, halve the plums, remove the stones, then cut each half into 4 wedges. Put the butter, ground almonds, sugar, flour, cinnamon if using, and egg in a food processor and whiz to a smooth, creamy batter. Spoon into the flan tin and level the surface. Nestle the plum wedges into the mixture, placing them skin-side up.

4 Bake the flan for 30–35 minutes until risen, firm and golden brown. Remove from the oven and brush with the jam glaze while still warm. Leave to cool slightly in the tin, then unmould and slide on to a flat plate. Serve warm, cut into wedges.

VARIATION

Instead of the plums, use 6–8 French mi-cuit Agen prunes for the filling. First soak them in hot Earl Grey tea to cover for about 2–3 hours, then drain, stone if necessary, and cut the prunes into quarters. Place in a small bowl and sprinkle with 2–3 tablespoons Armagnac or Cognac. Leave to macerate overnight, then drain and use in the same way as the plum wedges.

500g Pâte Sucrée (page 191)
4 large, ripe dark red plums
125g unsalted butter, softened to room temperature
125g ground almonds
125g caster sugar
25g plain flour
1 teaspoon ground cinnamon (optional)
1 large free-range egg
3–4 tablespoons apricot or plum jam glaze (see below)

JAM GLAZE This gives a tempting, glossy sheen to a home baked tart. Simply warm about 4 tablespoons apricot or plum jam in a small pan with 1–2 tablespoons water and a squeeze of lemon juice until the jam melts. Heat until bubbling, stir briefly, then pass through a sieve, rubbing gently with the back of a wooden spoon. We make up a large batch of this glaze and store it in a screw-topped jar in the fridge ready to use.

passion fruit and orange tart

This tart is an elegant variation of the classic French tarte au citron. For an intensely fruity taste, I first boil the passion fruit and orange juice to reduce and concentrate the flavour. A thin whisper of dark chocolate lines the tart case, adding a hint of contrasting flavour; it also helps to prevent the creamy passion fruit filling softening the pastry. Serve cut into wedges, with a scoop of vanilla ice cream if you like. **SERVES 6–8**

1 Halve the passion fruit, scoop out the pulp into a saucepan and add the orange juice. Bring to the boil and boil until reduced by half. Pass through a sieve into a jug, rubbing with the back of a wooden spoon to extract the juice from the passion fruit seeds. You should have around 250ml; set aside to cool.

2 Roll out the pastry as thinly as possible, ideally to a 3mm thickness, on a lightly floured surface. Lift it on the rolling pin into a 21–22cm flan tin that is about 2cm deep with a removable base. Press the pastry well into the sides and leave about 1cm overhanging the top edge. Don't worry if the pastry cracks as you press it in, simply pinch the dough together to mend the cracks. Prick the base, line with greaseproof paper or foil and baking beans, then rest in the fridge for 20 minutes. Meanwhile, preheat the oven to 200°C, Gas 6.

3 Stand the flan tin on a baking sheet and bake blind for 15 minutes. Remove the paper or foil and beans and return the flan case to the oven for 5 minutes until the base is pale golden and crisp. Using a sharp knife, carefully trim the overhanging pastry until neatly level with the top of the tin. Set aside to cool and lower the oven setting to 150°C, Gas 2.

4 Meanwhile, break up the chocolate and melt in a small heatproof bowl over a pan of simmering water, or in the microwave on medium for about 2 minutes. Allow the chocolate to cool until tepid, but still runny.

5 Using a pastry brush, spread the chocolate evenly and thinly over the base and up the sides of the pastry case, ideally while the pastry is still slightly warm. Allow to cool and set.

6 For the filling, beat the reduced fruit juice, sugar, cream and eggs together in a bowl until smooth, then strain through a sieve into a jug. Stand the flan tin on a baking sheet and place on the middle shelf of the oven, pulling the shelf out as far as it is safe to do. Pour the filling into the case until it reaches the top. Carefully push the oven shelf and tart back into the oven and bake for 35–40 minutes until the top forms a light crust and appears to be lightly set, although it may still be slightly soft in the centre.

7 Carefully remove the tart from the oven and allow to cool. The filling will continue to firm up as it cools. Chill until ready to serve, then carefully unmould and cut into wedges.

6 ripe, wrinkled passion fruits
350ml fresh orange juice
350g Pâte Sucrée (page 191)
40g dark chocolate
250g caster sugar
200ml double cream
6 medium free-range eggs

CHEF'S SECRET For a light caramelised finish, dust the chilled tart with a light even layer of sifted icing sugar, then immediately caramelise by waving a cook's blow-torch over the surface.

perfect scones

I despair that so many people have only ever tasted mass produced scones. Homemade ones are so much better and it takes very little time to mix the dough, pat it out, shape and bake. I find that baking scones at a lower temperature than is usual ensures that they remain soft on the outside, yet still rise beautifully. Scones are always best eaten fresh and warm from the oven, spilt and buttered – with or without clotted cream and homemade strawberry jam. **MAKES 8–10**

250g self-raising flour

1 teaspoon baking powder

good pinch of fine sea salt

45g unsalted butter, softened

1 tablespoon caster sugar, plus extra
  to dust

50g sultanas

1 large free-range egg

100ml ice-cold milk, plus extra
  to glaze

1 Preheat the oven to 180°C, Gas 4. Line a baking sheet with baking parchment.

2 Sift the flour, baking powder and salt together into a large bowl. Add the butter in little pieces and rub it in using the tips of your fingers and lifting the flour up high so you aerate it. When the butter is incorporated the mixture should look like fine breadcrumbs. Stir in the caster sugar, then the sultanas.

2 In another bowl, beat the egg with the milk. Pour about three quarters into the flour mixture and quickly mix together with a large table knife, adding extra egg and milk mix as necessary to give a soft but not sticky dough. Do not over-mix – the quicker and lighter the mixing the higher your scones will rise.

3 Tip the dough on to a lightly floured surface and very gently roll with a rolling pin or pat out with your fingers to a 2–2.5cm thickness. Using a 6cm cutter, press out as many rounds as you can. Gently re-shape and lightly roll the trimmings to cut out a couple more rounds if you can.

4 Place the rounds on the lined baking sheet, brush the tops with milk and sprinkle lightly with extra sugar. Bake for 20–25 minutes until risen and golden brown. To check that the scones are ready, lightly squeeze the sides of one – the dough should be springy. Slide off on to a wire rack and cool. Eat the scones within an hour or so of baking, while still warm.

VARIATIONS

Omit the sultanas and add 1 teaspoon ground cinnamon or mixed spice to the flour. Or, for savoury scones, omit the sugar and sultanas, mix in 50g finely grated mature Cheddar or Parmesan and $\frac{1}{2}$ teaspoon powdered English mustard and sprinkle the tops with a little more grated cheese before baking.

COOK'S TIP To save time, simply pat the dough out to a 2.5cm thick square with your hands, keeping the edges straight, then cut into squares. Alternatively, pat the dough into a 2.5cm thick round and score the top into 8 wedges. Bake for about 25 minutes, then cut on cooling.

lemon and vanilla kugelhopf

Similar to a classic Genoese sponge, this is a truly multi-purpose cake mixture, which can be used in a variety of ways to suit different occasions. You can bake it in a kugelhopf mould (a fluted tin with a funnel centre) or a round deep tin to slice and fill with whipped crème fraîche. Or, to serve as a dessert, bake the mixture in a Swiss roll tin and cut out small rounds to sandwich with crushed fruits and whipped cream. Alternatively, you can bake it in Madeleine trays or bun tins. Use an electric mixer with a whisk attachment if you have one. **SERVES 10**

4 large unwaxed lemons, scrubbed

100g butter, plus 10g extra to
   grease tin

320g plain flour, plus extra to dust

2 teaspoons baking powder

5 medium free-range eggs

350g caster sugar

1 vanilla pod

150ml single cream

To serve:

icing sugar, to dust

summer berries, such as
   strawberries and raspberries

whipped cream

1 Finely grate the zest from the lemons and set aside. Melt all the butter until just runny and cool until tepid. Sift together the flour and baking powder.

2 Use 1 tablespoon of the melted butter to grease a 22cm kugelhopf ring mould, then dust liberally with flour and tap out the excess. Preheat the oven to 160°C, Gas 3.

3 Put the eggs and sugar into an electric mixer bowl. Slit the vanilla pod open, scrape out the seeds using the tip of a small sharp knife, and add them to the sugar. Beat, using a whisk attachment, until pale golden and thick enough to leave a trail when the beaters are lifted. This may take up to 10 minutes.

4 Remove the bowl from the mixer and gently fold in the flour and lemon zest, using a large metal spoon. Pour the cream and runny butter down the sides of the bowl and, using a figure-of-eight motion gently incorporate into the mixture, retaining as much of the volume as possible.

5 Gently scoop the mixture into the prepared cake tin and bake in the centre of the oven for 50 minutes to 1 hour, or until a skewer inserted in the middle comes out clean. The top should be springy when pressed and the cake will have started to come away very slightly from the edge of the tin.

6 Invert on to a wire rack and leave to cool with the tin over the cake for 10 minutes, then remove the tin and leave to cool completely. Dust with sifted icing sugar and serve in thin wedges, with summer berries and whipped cream.

VARIATIONS

Bake the mixture in a lined and greased deep 25cm round cake tin for 50–60 minutes. After cooling, split and fill with cream and crushed fruits, then dust with icing sugar to serve. Alternatively, bake the mixture in a shallow Swiss roll tin for about 20 minutes. After cooling, trim the edges and cut out rounds. Sandwich together with whipped cream flavoured with Stock Syrup infused with lemon grass (page 164) and crushed raspberries.

CHEF'S SECRET This cake has a rich buttery flavour with a light sponge texture, achieved by whisking eggs and sugar vigorously to incorporate as much air as possible, then carefully folding in melted runny butter and cream to keep the mixture light.

dark, rich carrot cake

This wonderfully moist cake from the Connaught repertoire takes me back to my childhood and memories of my mother's tasty carrot cake. Not only is it easy to make and bake, it is really healthy being dairy free and high in fibre, vitamins and minerals. So, Mum, this one's for you! **SERVES 8–10**

1 Preheat the oven to 150°C, Gas 2. Grease a 1kg loaf tin and line the base with baking parchment. Sift the flour, spice and bicarbonate of soda together, then tip in the bran from the sieve if it won't rub through. Peel and coarsely grate the carrots; you should have around 200g. Set aside.

2 Beat 175g of the sugar with the oil and orange zest, using a large electric mixer or by hand, until smooth. Beat in the eggs, one by one, until light and creamy. Fold in the sifted flour mixture until smooth, then finally fold in the grated carrot, sultanas, coconut and chopped walnuts.

3 Turn the mixture into the prepared loaf tin and level the top. Stand the tin on a heavy baking sheet and bake for 1 hour 20–25 minutes. Meanwhile, gently heat the orange juice with the remaining sugar and lemon juice in a small saucepan until the sugar is dissolved.

4 To check that the cake is cooked, insert a metal skewer – it should come out clean. Also, the top should feel quite firm when pressed. Run a knife around the edges of the cake to loosen it. Prick holes all over the surface with a skewer, then slowly drizzle over the orangey syrup so it seeps into the holes and round the edges. Leave the cake in the tin until all the syrup is absorbed, then turn out and remove the base paper. Place on a wire rack and leave to cool completely. Store in an airtight cake tin until required. Serve cut into thick slices.

200g plain wholemeal flour

1 tablespoon ground mixed spice

1 teaspoon bicarbonate of soda

225g carrots

250g soft dark brown sugar

150ml sunflower oil

finely grated zest of 1 large orange

2 medium free-range eggs

110g sultanas

50g desiccated coconut

50g chopped walnuts

juice of ½ large orange

1 tablespoon lemon juice

CHEF'S TIP Pouring a citrus syrup over this cake as it cools makes it more moist and imparts a tangy flavour. The crust needs to be well punctured with a skewer to enable the syrup to soak in.

chocolate truffle ravioli

Brioche dough is highly versatile. These little brioche 'doughnuts' are filled with a chocolate ganache, which melts in the centre and oozes out as you bite into them. Quite divine as a chic dessert or treat with coffee. **MAKES 20–24**

Ganache filling:

80g dark chocolate (60% cocoa
    solids)

40g unsalted butter

3 tablespoons double cream

Brioche dough:

10g fresh yeast or 2 teaspoons dried
    active yeast

150ml tepid milk

25g caster sugar, plus extra to dust

400g strong plain flour

2 teaspoons fine sea salt

40g unsalted butter

2 medium free-range eggs, beaten

vegetable oil, for deep-frying

1 First make the ganache. Break up the chocolate and place in a heatproof bowl with the butter and cream. Place over a pan of gently simmering water and stir until melted and smooth. Remove and cool, then chill until solid.

2 Using a small melon baller, scoop out 20–24 balls of ganache; they don't need to be perfect spheres. Chill until required.

3 To make the brioche dough, if using fresh yeast mix with the tepid milk and a pinch of the sugar. If using dried yeast, whisk the granules into the milk with a pinch of sugar and set aside until it starts to froth.

4 Meanwhile, sift the flour and salt into a large bowl, set on a damp cloth to hold it steady. Rub in the butter until the mixture resembles fine breadcrumbs, then mix in the remaining caster sugar. Make a well in the centre. Pour in the yeasty milk and all but 2 tablespoons of the beaten egg. Mix to a dough and shape into a ball with your hands.

5 Knead on a lightly floured surface for about 8 minutes until the dough is smooth and elastic. Place in an oiled large bowl and turn the dough to coat in the oil. Cover the bowl with cling film and leave in a warm place until the dough has doubled in size.

6 Knock back the dough, then knead until smooth. Roll out on a lightly floured surface to the thickness of a £1 coin. Using a 5 or 6cm cutter, press out 40–48 rounds, re-rolling if necessary and shape the ravioli (see below). Rest in the fridge for 15 minutes.

7 When ready to serve, half-fill a deep saucepan or deep-fat fryer with oil and heat to 180°C. Have ready a shallow bowl of caster sugar, and kitchen paper for draining. Deep-fry the filled dough balls, about 4–6 at a time, for 1½ minutes until golden brown. Drain on kitchen paper for a minute, then toss in the sugar to coat. Cool slightly, but serve still warm so the chocolate centre is still melted.

TO SHAPE THE RAVIOLI
Place a chocolate ball in the centre of half the rounds. Brush around the edges with the reserved egg, thinned with a little water. Cover with the remaining rounds and mould the dough around the chocolate with your fingers. Press the edges together well to seal. You will now have 20–24 little flying saucers!

Stocks, sauces and dressings

I am frequently complemented on the way I get so much flavour into my dishes, yet manage to keep them light in texture. So, what is my secret? The answer is simple. I start at the beginning of a recipe, adding essences from raw and basic ingredients with stocks, infusions and sauces.

Time and heat are good allies. I concentrate flavours by reducing liquids through boiling – what goes up in steam is simply water – the flavour is left behind. To create flavoured oils, again, I use heat to extract the flavour from fresh herbs, garlic or chilli, for example. These flavours are readily absorbed and I use the infused oils to enhance vegetables, salad dressings and so on. You will notice that infusions and reductions feature in many of my dishes.

All stocks are made freshly in my kitchens. Meat stock is prepared with fresh veal, beef or lamb bones according to the dish. We use fresh carcasses for chicken stock, and select white fish bones carefully for fish stocks. Using fresh stocks makes a big difference to a sauce or soup, especially if the stock is the main ingredient. You won't need to make it that often. Just make up a good quantity and freeze it in convenient amounts, say 250–300ml. One point to note is that we do not add salt to stocks in case we over season them. That comes later.

Stocks, sauces and dressings are the essential basic elements in my recipes. If you spend time getting these right, the rest of the dish will follow.

court bouillon

A court bouillon is a poaching liquor used for whole fish, lobster and crab. It imparts flavour and acidity to give fish and seafood a subtle piquancy. I find it is worth the time to make up a court bouillon for simple poaching because of the added value in terms of flavour. **MAKES ABOUT 2 LITRES**

2 leeks, roughly chopped

2 carrots, roughly chopped

1 celery stick, roughly chopped

1 large onion, roughly chopped

2 medium shallots, roughly chopped

½ fennel bulb, chopped

3 garlic cloves (unpeeled)

1 large sprig each thyme, tarragon, basil and parsley, tied together

2 litres water

½ teaspoon white peppercorns

10g rock salt

1 lemon, sliced

1 star anise

200ml dry white wine

1 Put all the vegetables and garlic into a large stock pot with the bunch of herbs and cover with the cold water. Bring to the boil. Add the rest of the ingredients, return to a simmer and cook gently for about 30 minutes.

2 Strain the court bouillon through a colander lined with wet muslin into a deep bowl. Discard the vegetables and flavourings.

3 Cool the liquor unless using straightaway. It can be kept, covered, in the fridge for up to 3 days, or frozen.

CHEF'S TIP Court bouillon can be strained and reused up to three times, provided that it is strained again and chilled or frozen in between, then brought to the boil before use. Don't be tempted to use leftover court bouillon as a stock for soups and sauces, as it is too acidic.

fish stock

For a fine flavoured fish stock with a light colour, choose sole or turbot bones, plus heads. Ask your fishmonger if he has any to spare, even if you are not buying sole or turbot at the time, or give him notice to put some aside for you. You will need around 1.5kg. If turbot or sole aren't possibilities, you can use the bones of other white fish, but not oily fish like salmon. Fish stock is essential, I would say, for true fish soups or fish veloutés. **MAKES ABOUT 1.5 LITRES**

1 Prepare the bones and heads. If using the head of a large fish, remove the eyes and gills, then chop the head in half. Avoid using the skin too, if possible. Rinse away any blood from backbones under cold running water, as this might give the stock a bitter taste. Roughly chop the bones so they will fit into the pan.

2 Put all the vegetables into a stock pot with the olive oil, then heat until they start to sizzle. Cover with a lid and sweat gently over a low heat for about 15 minutes, shaking the pan occasionally.

3 Stir in the fish bones and wine and cook until the wine evaporates almost totally away. Now pour in the water, add the herbs, lemon and peppercorns, and bring to the boil over a medium high heat.

4 As the liquid boils gently you will note a scum forms. This is simply due to fish proteins and is quite harmless. However, we skim it off with a wide skimming spoon so it does not make the stock cloudy.

5 Turn the heat down and simmer, uncovered, for 20 minutes – no longer or the stock may acquire a bitter taste from the bones. Turn off the heat and leave undisturbed for 10 minutes so the particles settle.

6 Line a large colander with wet muslin and set over a large bowl or smaller pan. Gently tip the liquid through the muslin. If it helps, remove the larger bones first with a slotted spoon. If you are not using the stock straightaway, cool then chill. You should have about 1.5 litres. Alternatively, you can boil the strained stock down to about 1 litre to concentrate the flavour.

about 1.5kg white fish bones and
  heads
1 leek, chopped
1 onion, chopped
1 celery stick, chopped
½ fennel bulb, chopped
2 garlic cloves (unpeeled)
100ml light olive oil (not extra virgin)
300ml dry white wine
2 litres water
2 sprigs each thyme and parsley, tied
  together
½ lemon, sliced
½ teaspoon white peppercorns

CHEF'S TIP Make a batch of stock, boil to concentrate and freeze in two 500ml containers. Don't forget to label, or you might mistake it for chicken or vegetable flavours. Unsalted stock should keep in the freezer for up to 3 months.

chicken stock

This is a good multi-purpose stock. We make chicken stock using fresh chicken carcasses delivered daily to the restaurants, but I appreciate these are not always available to home cooks. Instead, you can buy packs of cheap fresh chicken wings. Light chicken stock is used in soups and creamy veloutés, but we also use a dark (or brown) chicken stock for pork, lamb and game bird dishes. It is made in the same way as light chicken stock except that the carcasses are first roasted in a hot oven. This gives a depth of colour and flavour without an over-meaty taste. **MAKES 2 LITRES**

2kg raw chicken carcasses or bony
   chicken joints (such as wings or
   backs)
4 litres cold water
3 celery sticks, roughly chopped
2 leeks, roughly chopped
2 onions, roughly chopped
2 large carrots, roughly chopped
½ head garlic (unpeeled)
1 large thyme sprig

1 Put the chicken carcasses into a stock pot, cover with the water and bring to the boil. Using a slotted spoon, skim off any white scum.

2 Add the chopped vegetables to the pan along with the garlic and thyme. Return to the boil, then turn down the heat to a gentle simmer and cook, uncovered for about 3 hours, skimming occasionally if necessary.

3 Strain the stock through a colander lined with wet muslin into a large bowl. Discard all the debris. If you want a stronger stock, return the liquid to the pan and continue boiling until reduced by half. Cool, chill and use within 3 days, or freeze in 500ml quantities.

BROWN CHICKEN STOCK We use this stock to give a sauce some depth of flavour and a light colour. Follow the recipe above, but first toss the bones or bony joints in about 100ml light olive oil to coat, then place in a roasting tin and roast at 200°C, Gas 6 for 15–20 minutes turning once or twice until nicely browned. Continue as above.

vegetable nage

This vegetable stock is one of the secrets of our light, yet full flavoured sauces. It isn't simply made by boiling all the ingredients together. Infusion is the secret. The vegetables are simmered briefly, then fresh herbs are added and the nage is left to infuse for a good day before straining. This is the stock we use for our vegetarian dishes and light vegetable soups. Occasionally I combine vegetable nage with some fish or light chicken stock in a sauce. **MAKES ABOUT 1.5 LITRES**

1 Put all the vegetables, garlic, lemon, peppercorns, bay leaf and star anise into a large saucepan or stock pot with the water. Bring to the boil, lower the heat and simmer for 10 minutes.

2 Remove the pan from the heat, push in the bouquet of herbs and stir in the wine. Cool to allow the vegetables and herbs to infuse the liquid with their delicate flavours.

3 Spoon the cooled vegetables and flavourings into a large jug or other suitable container and tip in all of the liquid. Cover and infuse in the fridge for 24 hours or so, then strain through a muslin-lined colander into another jug or bowl. Keep covered in the fridge for up to 3 days until ready to use. Alternatively, freeze in smaller amounts, remembering to label the containers.

3 onions, roughly chopped
1 leek, roughly chopped
2 celery sticks, roughly chopped
6 carrots, roughly chopped
1 head of garlic, split in half
1 lemon, roughly chopped
½ teaspoon white peppercorns
½ teaspoon pink peppercorns
1 small bay leaf
4 star anise
2 litres cold water
1 sprig each tarragon, basil, coriander, thyme, parsley and chervil, tied together
200ml dry white wine

velouté

A good velouté requires fresh stock – use chicken or fish stock, or vegetable nage depending on the recipe. This sauce gets its depth of flavour by boiling down the wine, stock and cream in stages. Occasionally we whisk in a knob of ice cold butter to give the sauce a sheen. **MAKES ABOUT 500ml**

10g butter

3 shallots, finely chopped

200ml dry white wine

200ml Noilly Prat or dry vermouth

400ml Fish Stock (page 209),
   Chicken Stock (page 210) or
   Vegetable Nage (page 211)

200ml double cream

200ml single cream

sea salt and freshly ground white
   pepper

1 Heat the butter in a wide saucepan, stir in the shallots then sauté gently for about 15 minutes until softened but not coloured. Deglaze with the wine and vermouth, then boil for about 7 minutes until reduced by half.

2 Pour in the stock or nage, return to the boil, stirring, and continue to boil until reduced by half.

3 Now add the two creams, bring back to a gentle boil and simmer until the sauce is the consistency of pouring cream. Season to taste, then strain the sauce through a fine sieve. It should by now be smooth and glossy.

THYME VELOUTÉ

Use vegetable nage and proceed as above, adding 3 large thyme sprigs with the stock. If desired, strip the leaves from another small thyme sprig and stir these into the sauce just before serving.

CHEF'S TIP You will find that even fresh vegetables, wine, bones and herbs used to make stocks and sauces have some natural salty flavour and this will be concentrated by boiling and reducing. This is why I always season a sauce at the end.

red wine sauce

Red wine sauces are usually associated with red meats, but we also use them for chicken dishes and, surprisingly perhaps, certain full flavoured fish like salmon, monkfish or turbot. Depending on the intended purpose, you can use either fish stock or light chicken stock as the base – both work well. Freeze any sauce that you don't need now for later use. Resist the temptation to use a cheap red wine, a medium quality Cabernet Sauvignon or softer Merlot wine will give a far better result. **MAKES 400ml**

1 First, pour the red wine into a wide shallow pan and boil down until reduced by three quarters to a rich syrupy liquid, about 200ml.

2 Heat the olive oil in another pan and sauté the shallots for 5 minutes until they soften and start to caramelise, then add the five spice powder, peppercorns, thyme and bay leaf. Cook for another 5 minutes, then deglaze with the sherry vinegar.

3 Now add the reduced wine and the stock. Bring to the boil and boil rapidly for about 10–15 minutes until reduced by half. Carefully skim off any scum or fat from the surface using a ladle.

4 Slowly pour the hot liquid through a sieve lined with wet muslin. Repeat this process once more to clarify the sauce even further, then season to taste.

75cl bottle red wine

2 tablespoons olive oil

4 large shallots, sliced

1 teaspoon five spice powder

12 black peppercorns

1 thyme sprig

1 small bay leaf

1 tablespoon sherry vinegar

750ml light Chicken Stock (page 210) or Fish Stock (page 209)

sea salt and freshly ground black pepper

pan jus gravy

This is a quick sauce using the natural jus (or pan juices) from cooked meat, poultry or fish. The jus is enriched with a glass of wine, but you don't need to open a bottle especially, a splash of Noilly Prat from the storecupboard will do. If you haven't any homemade stock to hand, use a bought tub of fresh stock.

MAKES ABOUT 170ml

pan 'jus' from cooking a steak, chicken joint or fish fillet

1–2 tablespoons olive oil

1 shallot, finely chopped

1 thyme sprig

1 teaspoon white wine or red wine vinegar

1 glass (about 175ml) red or white wine

about 150ml fresh stock, or water mixed with 1 teaspoon bouillon powder

1 tablespoon crème fraîche or double cream

sea salt and freshly ground black pepper

1 Put the roasting tin (or other pan the meat or fish has been cooked in) on the hob over a low heat. Add the olive oil, shallot and thyme, and cook gently, stirring to scrape up the sediment, for about 3 minutes until softened.

2 Deglaze the pan with the vinegar, then pour in the wine. Bring to the boil and boil until reduced by half.

3 Now add the stock, return to the boil and reduce by a third. Whisk in the crème fraîche or cream and cook for another minute or so. Check the seasoning and pour through a sieve into a jug.

classic pesto

We make fresh pesto to use as garnish, often thinning it down with vinaigrette or water and decanting it into a 'squirty' plastic bottle, so we can easily swirl it on to plates of pasta, soups, etc. Purists would use a pestle and mortar, but we make pesto in a blender or food processor. Pine nuts soon turn rancid, so buy fresh ones rather than use a pack you find lurking at the back of a cupboard – shame to spoil good olive oil and fresh, fragrant basil. **MAKES ABOUT 300ml**

1 Place the pine nuts, garlic and Parmesan in a food processor and whiz until you have a fine crumbly mixture.
2 With the motor still running, feed in the basil leaves through the chute, then slowly trickle in the olive oil. Process until you have a smooth purée.
3 Spoon the pesto into a screw-topped jar, seal and store in the fridge for up to 1 week. Or if you like, thin the pesto with 3–4 tablespoons cold water or vinaigrette and pour into a plastic bottle with a squirty top before refrigerating for up to 1 week.

50g pine nuts
50g garlic cloves, peeled and roughly chopped
50g Parmesan cheese, finely grated
30g basil leaves
120ml extra virgin olive oil

CHEF'S TIP Fresh pesto will keep better in a screw-topped jar if you pour a thin layer of olive oil over the surface before refrigerating.

herb oils

I love to infuse olive oil with herbs and other flavourings to trickle over hot vegetables or grilled fish, chicken and chargrilled vegetables. Infused oils add instant flavour and richness with little effort. You can also use them in vinaigrette dressings, diluted half and half with pure olive oil. It is important to heat the oil to at least 90°C to destroy any airborne bacteria in herb sprigs and other flavourings, then bottle and seal while hot. This takes 2–3 minutes over a medium heat and does not affect the flavour of the oil. It is also a good idea to ensure the bottle is sterilised first either by putting it through a dishwasher cycle or heating it in a warm oven for 10 minutes. There is no need to use extra virgin olive oil for infusions, pure grade olive oil will suffice. **MAKES 250ml**

30g basil sprigs, including stalks
250ml pure olive oil (not extra virgin)

1 Wash the basil sprigs under cold running water, then pat dry between kitchen paper or spin in a salad spinner.

2 Heat the olive oil gently in a medium pan over a moderate heat to about 90°C; this takes about 3 minutes. Add the basil and stir gently until wilted. Leave on the heat for 1 minute, then remove.

3 Lift the basil sprigs into a clean, sterilised bottle, pushing them down with a skewer or chopstick. Then carefully pour in the heated oil. Seal immediately and cool. Store in a cool place out of direct sunlight. You can store the oil in the fridge, but expect it to go cloudy – this doesn't affect the flavour.

VARIATIONS
Rosemary Wash 3–4 sprigs of fresh rosemary, dry and proceed as above.
Sage Wash a good handful of fresh sage leaves, dry and proceed as above.
Red pepper Core, deseed and slice a medium red pepper. Sauté in 4 tablespoons of the above quantity of olive oil for 2–3 minutes until just softened. Then add the remaining oil and heat for another 2 minutes. Continue as above.
Garlic Sauté about 8 peeled, fat garlic cloves in a little of the olive oil to cover for 2 minutes, but do not allow to burn. Add the remaining oil and heat for another 2–3 minutes. Continue as above.
Chilli Infuse 4–6 whole dried chillies, according to taste in the oil as it heats. Or slice 3–4 large fresh chillies and lightly sauté in 3 tablespoons of the olive oil, then add the remaining oil and continue as above. For a milder flavour, deseed the chillies before slicing. Try combining chilli with 4 garlic cloves.

vinaigrette

We use vinaigrettes to dress a variety of dishes, not just salads. New potatoes, pasta and couscous, for example, are often tossed in a vinaigrette flavoured with chopped fresh herbs while still warm. But I also drizzle vinaigrette dressings over grilled fish, chicken and even sliced pan-fried liver and steaks, varying the oil and vinegar to suit the particular dish.

The base should always be a medium flavour pure or extra virgin olive oil, mixed with a more neutral oil such as groundnut or sunflower oil. You can replace part of either oil with a nut oil, but use sparingly – hazelnut and walnut oils can be very aromatic.

I use proportionally less vinegar to oil in my dressings than most classic recipes, simply because too much vinegar can overpower a dish. A quality white wine vinegar is fine, though you might like to experiment with different vinegars (see below). I also add fresh lemon juice for a fruity, citrus hint. Make a good quantity of vinaigrette and store in the fridge; shake or whisk before each use. **MAKES ABOUT 250ml**

100ml extra virgin olive oil

100ml groundnut oil

½ teaspoon Maldon sea salt, crushed

¼ teaspoon freshly ground white or black pepper

1 tablespoon lemon juice, or to taste

2 tablespoons white wine vinegar

1 Put all the ingredients into a jug or bowl and whisk together until emulsified.

2 Pour the vinaigrette into a clean bottle or jar and store in the fridge. Shake each time you use it.

VARIATIONS

Mustard and honey dressing Add 3 teaspoons coarse grain mustard with 1 teaspoon clear honey. Or for a vinaigrette with a subtle mustard flavour, just add a scant teaspoon of plain Dijon mustard (no honey).

Herb dressing Chopped fresh herbs can be added to the vinaigrette at the last minute before serving – not before as the bright green colour will turn to grey on storage. Add about 1 tablespoon chopped herbs to each 100ml of dressing. Chopped chervil, chives and parsley are all excellent in a dressing.

VINEGARS FOR DRESSINGS To vary the flavour, replace some or all of the white wine vinegar. Rice wine vinegar is lighter and slightly sweeter, or for a fuller, flavour with a hint of apple, include a little cider vinegar. Aged balsamic vinegar will impart a special character. Spanish sherry vinegar is one of my favourites, though it is quite strong, so a teaspoon is enough to lend a mellow flavour. Another Spanish vinegar, forvm agridulce de Cabernet Sauvignon is a blend of wine vinegar and grape juice that's almost syrupy and good enough to sip neat from a spoon.

mayonnaise

A freshly made mayonnaise is far superior to anything you can buy. It uses egg yolks to stabilise the emulsion and always remains thick and spoonable. If required, you can lighten a thick mayonnaise with vinaigrette, using at least 2 tablespoons mayonnaise to each 1 tablespoon vinaigrette. Note that raw egg yolks are used – choose the best organic eggs available.

Whisking a mayonnaise by hand will give the best result, but you can use a blender or food processor, using 1 whole egg and 1 yolk rather than 2 yolks, and slowly adding the oil through the chute while the motor is running. The mayo will be paler in colour and a little more runny. **MAKES ABOUT 300ml**

1 Put the egg yolks, wine vinegar, salt, pepper to taste, and mustard into a bowl. Stand this on a damp cloth to hold it steady. Using a balloon whisk, beat well until smooth and creamy. Now trickle in a few drops of oil from the tip of a teaspoon, whisking vigorously.

2 Continue to whisk in the oil drop by drop at first, then slowly increasing the amount you add to a slow, steady stream, making sure each addition is well incorporated before you add any more. This way you will achieve a thick mayonnaise.

3 Finally, add 1–2 tablespoons cold water to stabilise the emulsion. Taste and adjust the seasoning if necessary.

VARIATIONS

Garlic mayonnaise Peel 3–4 fat garlic cloves and blanch in boiling water for 1 minute or so, then crush and stir into the finished mayonnaise.

Red pepper mayonnaise This is superb with grilled Mediterranean fish, such as red mullet or sea bass. Make up the mayonnaise (as above) and set aside. Put 2 finely chopped large red peppers in a saucepan with 4–5 tablespoons olive oil and heat until sizzling. Add 1 thyme sprig and 1 tarragon sprig and cook gently, stirring once or twice, until soft but not browned, about 10 minutes. Remove the herbs and whiz in a blender or food processor until smooth and creamy. Pass though a sieve rubbing with the back of a wooden spoon. Cool, then stir into the mayonnaise and check the seasoning.

2 free-range organic egg yolks
1 teaspoon white wine vinegar
½ teaspoon sea salt
freshly ground white or black pepper
1 teaspoon English mustard powder
300ml groundnut oil or light olive oil
  (not extra virgin)

CHEF'S TIP If you are unlucky enough to find your mayonnaise does split, try this remedy. Whisk another egg yolk in a separate bowl with a pinch each of salt, pepper and mustard, then whisk in the split mixture. It should re-emulsify.

Index

Acknowledgements

I am a great believer in teamwork, and certainly no book with this much quality of information and presentation would be possible without it. Mark Sargeant (aka Sarge) is my main secret. He has gathered together the recipes from his Claridges kitchens and cheerfully made them up for the Saturday shoots, where they were beautifully photographed by the gorgeous Georgia Glynn Smith, having been art directed by Helen Lewis. Petite Helen may be, but her talent for design is great and one major reason for the continuing success of my previous books. On the words front I have to give credit to Roz Denny, tester-in-chief and wordsmith; and to Janet Illsley, the project editor, for pulling it all together on paper.

Three other important behind the scenes ladies were a major influence for making everything run like clockwork. My adorable wife, Tana for tolerating our weekly recipe meetings at home and for getting me out of bed for Saturday photo sessions; to Anne Furniss, the Publishing Director of Quadrille, for her inspiration and patience; and finally to my PA, Lynne Brenner, without whom I wouldn't know where to be when.